DETROIT PUBLIC LIBRARY
3 5674 05678183 5

P9-EMG-880

Love Warrior

ALSO BY GLENNON DOYLE MELTON

CARRY ON, WARRIOR
The Power of Embracing Your Messy, Beautiful Life

Love Warrior

Glennon Doyle Melton

Certain names and identifying characteristics have been changed, whether or not so noted in the text, and certain characters and events have been compressed or reordered.

For information, address Flatiron Books,
175 Fifth Avenue, New York, N.Y. 10010.

www.flatironbooks.com

Grateful acknowledgment is made for permission to reproduce from the following:

"Hero" words and music by Walter Afanasieff and Mariah Carey © 1993 WB Music Corp., Wallyworld Music, songs of Universal Inc. and Rye Songs. All rights on behalf of itself and Wallyworld Music. Administered by WB Music Corp. All rights for Rye Songs administered by Songs of Universal., Inc. All rights reserved. Used by permission of Alfred Music and Hal Leonard Corporation.

Designed by Kathryn Parise

The Library of Congress Cataloging-in-Publication Data
is available upon request.

ISBN 978-1-250-12854-6 (Oprah's Book Club edition)

Our books may be purchased in bulk for promotional, educational, or business use. Please contact your local bookseller or the Macmillan Corporate and Premium Sales Department at 1-800-221-7945, extension 5442, or by e-mail at MacmillanSpecialMarkets@macmillan.com.

First Oprah's Book Club Edition: September 2016

10 9 8 7 6 5 4 3 2 1

For Grandma Alice, whose fingers danced across those beads
and brought Mary to me

I am not afraid . . . I was born to do this.

—Joan of Arc

Prelude

It's almost time. My father and I stand at the edge of a long white carpet, laid just this morning over the freshly cut grass. Craig's childhood backyard is transformed by the start of fall and the promise this day holds. My shoulders are bare and I feel a chill, so I lift my face toward the sun. I squint and the sun, leaves, and sky melt together into a kaleidoscope of blue, green, and orange. The leaves, my soon-to-be husband, our families sitting upright in their dressiest clothes, and I—we are all turning into something else. We are becoming new. It's a becoming day.

We wait for the music to play so we can begin the short, forever walk toward Craig. I watch him, standing at the end of the carpet looking handsome, young, and nervous. He adjusts his tie, clasps his hands in front of him, then pushes them into his pockets. After a moment he pulls his hands back out, pressing them to his sides like a soldier. He looks untethered, and I wish I could go to him now and hold his restless hands. But my hands are occupied: One is in my father's hand and the other is on my belly. I'm a bridge between my past and future. While I watch Craig, the guests turn to watch me. I feel embarrassed by their attention—fraudulent, like I'm pretending to be a bride. My dress is too tight around my waist and I'm wearing fake eyelashes, a rhinestone tiara, and heels like stilts. I am more costumed than I am dressed. But this is what a bride is supposed to look like, and since the day I decided to become sober and a mother, I've been trying to become who I'm supposed to be.

Our music begins and my dad squeezes my hand. I look up at his face. He smiles and says, "Here we go, sweetheart." He wraps his arm around my arm so that all of him is holding up all of me. As I walk with my father I start to feel dizzy, so I shift my eyes toward my sister. She is standing to the left of the minister in a flaming red dress. Her hair is pinned up, her back is straight, and her certainty is a flood that drowns out my fear. If there is anyone in charge here, it's her. She is smiling at me, and her fierce, steady eyes say: *If you keep walking—I'm here to stand beside you. If you turn around and run, I'll follow and we'll never look back. Whatever you do right now, Sister, you're fine. I'm here.* This is what she has been telling me since she was born. *You are fine. I am here.*

I keep walking. When we reach the end of the carpet, the minister says, "Who presents this woman to be married?" My dad answers, "Her mother and I do." My father passes my hand to Craig, who accepts it because that is what he's supposed to do. Then my dad is gone and Craig and I are facing each other and holding each other's shaking hands. Our hands are a trembling pile. I look down and wonder which one of us will steady the other. We need a third person to still our hands. I look at my sister, but she can't help now. There is no third person. This is what marriage is.

When it's time to say our vows, I tell Craig that he is my proof that God knows me and loves me. Craig nods and then vows to put me before all others for the rest of his life. I look into his eyes and accept his promise on behalf of me and our baby. The minister says, "I now pronounce you: Mr. and Mrs. Melton." It's done. I am a new person. Mrs. Melton. I hope I will be better as her. I hope I become. That is the hope of everyone in the backyard.

I set out to write the story of my marriage. The first time I wrote it, I started with the wedding day, because that's when I thought marriage began. This assumption was my mistake.

We'll get back to my wedding day and all the terrible magic that followed, but for now, let's begin at the beginning. It's our only choice, it turns out.

PART ONE

1

I WAS LOVED. If love could prevent pain, I'd never have suffered. My leather baby book with *Glennon* branded on the front is one long poem written by my father and filled with pictures of my tender-faced mother holding my pink, flaky, braceleted hand. About my birth, my father wrote:

It really wasn't
a cry
That first noise
It was a fanfare
Announcing a marvel
That will never
Be
Repeated
There are no satin sheets
There are no handmaidens

No emissaries with jewels
No trumpets or announcements
Where are they!
Don't they know what
Happened here?!
A princess has arrived.

I was loved. Just like my daughter is loved. And still, one evening, she sat on the edge of my bed, looked up at me with naked brown eyes, and said, "I'm big, Mama. I'm bigger than the other girls. Why am I different? I want to be small again." Her words came out jagged, like she hated to break this to me, like she was ashamed to reveal her hidden truth. I took in her tears, pigtails, lip gloss, and the dirt on her hands—left over from climbing the banyan tree in our front yard. I scanned my mind for a response worthy of her, but there was nothing to find. Everything I'd learned about bodies, womanhood, power, and pain scattered upon hearing how my little girl said the word *big*. Like big was her curse, her irrefutable condition, her secret, her fall from grace. Like big was something inevitably unfolding *inside of her* that threatened her contract with the world.

My daughter was not asking: How will I deal with my body size? My daughter was asking: *How will I survive being this particular type of person in this particular type of world? How will I stay small like the world wants me to? And if I keep growing, how will anyone love me?* I looked at my daughter and I did not say *But you do not look big, honey*. She didn't, but neither do I. I've never looked big a day in my life. No matter. My daughter and I pay attention. We know what the world wants from us. We know we must decide whether to stay small, quiet, and uncomplicated or allow ourselves to grow as big, loud, and complex as we were made to be. Every girl must decide whether to be true to herself or true to the world. Every girl must decide whether to settle for adoration or fight for love. There on the bed, in her pigtails and pain, my daughter was me—the little girl I once was, the woman I am now, still struggling to answer the questions: *How can I be expansive and free and still be loved? Am I going to be a lady or am I going to be fully human? Do I trust the unfolding and continue to grow, or do I shut all of this down so I fit?*

~

I am four years old and my father is a football coach at our neighborhood high school. On game night, my mom bundles me up in a fluffy coat, earmuffs, and mittens. When she's done, she kneels in front of me and admires her work. She is pleased. She moves her hands to my cheeks, pulls my face toward hers, and kisses my nose. Together we wrap my baby sister, Amanda, in a puffy snowsuit. Amanda is our gift, and my mom and I spend all day wrapping and unwrapping her. When she's dressed, we take turns leaning over and kissing her cheeks while she kicks and giggles—her arms jutting straight out from her sides like a starfish.

We pile into our van, drive to the high school, and listen as leaves crunch under our boots during our walk toward the stadium. As we climb the popcorn-littered stairs, the drum of the marching band fills my chest, the smell of hot dogs fills my lungs, and the roar of the crowd fills my head. The night is thumping chaos, but my mittened hand is safe inside my mother's and she guides me forward. When we reach the entrance, the ticket ladies smile, put their hands over their hearts, and say, "Aren't you three the most precious things?" They wave us in, because we are the coach's girls, so we don't have to pay. Mom and I smile at the ladies, say *thank you,* and together we join the crowd under the bright stadium lights. When they see us, the students and parents collectively hush and step aside. A path appears. Quiet reverence is the world's response to my mother's beauty. When people see her, they pause and wait, full of hope, until her eyes rest upon them. Her eyes always do. My mother takes her time with people. Strangers give her their attention and she returns it. She is a queen who reigns with kindness. This is why people stare. They look because she's lovely, but they stare because she's love. I am always studying my mother and I am always watching other people watch my mother. *She is such a beautiful child,* strangers say to my mother daily. I have to learn what to do because beauty is a responsibility. People expect so much of it, it seems.

My childhood beauty is apparent in pictures: golden brown ringlets to my waist, porcelain skin, a smile as wide as the horizon, and bright hazel eyes. When strangers admire me, I practice returning their attention. I understand that beauty is a form of kindness. It is for giving away, and I try to be generous. In an attempt to maintain balance, my parents often remind me that I'm smart. I'm an early reader and, at four, converse like an adult. But I soon realize that smart is more complicated than beautiful. Strangers come close and pat my curls, but when I speak to them with confidence and clarity, their eyes widen and they pull back. They are drawn in by my smile but repelled by my boldness. They recover quickly by laughing, but the pulling away is done. I have felt it. They wanted to adore me and I complicated things by inserting myself into their experience of me. I begin to understand that beauty warms people and smart cools people. I also understand that being loved for beauty is a tenuous situation for a girl. Years later, when I become less beautiful, when I no longer have regal ringlets to pat or perfect skin to admire, when I'm no longer small and simple and precious, I wonder how I'll ever be worthy of offering or receiving love. Losing my beauty will feel like a fall from grace, rendering me useless. It will be as if I have not kept my end of the deal and the whole world is disappointed in me. Without beauty, what do I have left to warm people with?

But for now, the three of us are still perfect. We snuggle into the stands and cheer for our team together. When the game is over, I run onto the field because my dad is looking for me, always looking for me. I run through the players' padded legs toward my father and he lifts me up above his head. His players step aside to give us room. We spin until the stadium lights and the crowd blend together and the whole world is a blur. All that's clear is my dad below me. He puts me down, and while I steady myself I see that my mom and sister have made their way to us. As she approaches, my mom shines all her brilliance at my dad. She is brighter and more powerful than all the stadium lights combined. My dad hugs her with both arms and then takes our starfish baby and kisses her cheeks. The four of us are an island. This celebration happens after every game, whether we've won or lost. We are my dad's victory. We turn and process out through the crowd—no longer an island, now a parade—and people smile and wave and the four of us hold hands and sing the high school's fight song all the way back to the van.

~

I'm ten years old and trying to disappear into the corner of the velour couch in my grandmother's living room. My cousins chase each other from room to room, a tornado of squeals and skin. It's summer and most of them are wearing bathing suits, as if that's easy. Their bodies are light and wispy and they seem to float and flit together, in a unit—like a school of fish. They play together but playing requires a loss of self-consciousness and togetherness requires a sense of belonging. I have neither, so I can't join them. I am not a fish. I am heavy and solitary and separate, like a whale. This is why I stay sunken into the couch and watch.

As I clutch my now-empty bowl of potato chips and lick the salt off my fingers, an aunt passes by and notices me. She looks from me to my cousins and says, "Why don't you want to play, Glennon?" She's noticed that I don't belong. I feel ashamed. "I'm just watching," I say. She smiles and with kind amusement says, "I like your eye shadow." My hand goes to my face as I remember the purple eye shadow my cousin Caren applied that morning. On the car ride from our Virginia home to Ohio, excitement swelled in my chest because this would be the year I'd return a different girl. During this trip, Caren would make me over, change me into someone who looked like her, smelled like her, flitted like her. She would make me beautiful again. So that morning I sat on Caren's bedroom floor surrounded by curling irons and makeup, waiting to be transformed. When she finished, she held up a mirror and I tried to smile while my heart sank. My eyelids were smeared with purple and my cheeks were pink, but I just looked like me wearing my cousin's makeup. And that is why my aunt looks amused instead of impressed. I smile and say, "I was just about to wash it off." I put my bowl down and pull myself up and off the couch.

I climb my grandmother's stairs, walk into the bathroom, and lock the door behind me. I decide to take a bath, because the bathtub is my hiding place. I start the water and the downstairs voices fade. When the tub fills, I peel off my clothes, climb in, and float there for a while. Then I close my eyes and sink beneath the surface. I open my eyes to my underneath, underwater world—so quiet, so far away, so safe. My hair swirls around my shoulders and I reach up to touch it. It feels like silk, and I imagine I look just like a mermaid under here. I come up for air and then back under, back underneath. Eventually the water gets cold, so I let it drain out slowly and watch my body reappear. There it is again. I can never keep myself from reemerging. I start to feel heavier and heavier against the porcelain tub, as if gravity is increasing exponentially, as if I am being sucked toward the center of the earth. The water is only inches deep now and my thighs are spread out wide and huge and I wonder, *Is there another girl in the world this massive? Has anyone ever felt this heavy?* Eventually I'm pinned to the bottom of the dry tub—naked, exposed, beached. Being underneath never lasts. I pull myself out, dry off, get dressed, and go back downstairs. I stop in the kitchen to refill my bowl of chips before I settle back into the couch.

The television is on, turned to a show about a woman thirty years older than I. She kisses her children good night, climbs into bed with her husband, and lies with her eyes open until he falls asleep. Then she climbs out of bed and walks quietly out of the bedroom and into the kitchen. She stops at the counter and picks up a magazine. The camera zooms in on the skeletal blond cover girl. The woman puts down the magazine and walks to the freezer. She pulls out a carton of ice cream and a large spoon and she starts eating the ice cream, frantically at first, spoonful after spoonful, like she's starving. I have never seen anyone eat like this before. She eats the way I want to eat, like an animal. Eventually the madness on the woman's face is replaced by a faraway look. She keeps eating, but robotically now. I look at her and with shame and joy I think, *She's just like me. She's going underneath.* She finishes the carton, wraps it in a bag, and shoves it to the bottom of the trash. Then she walks into the bathroom, locks the door, leans over the toilet, and vomits up all of the ice cream. The process looks painful, but afterward she sits on the floor and seems relieved. I am stunned. I think, *This is what I've been missing: the relief. This is how to disappear without getting bigger. This is how to make the underneath last.*

Within a few months, I'm bingeing and purging several times a day. Every time I sense my unbelonging, my unworthiness—every time my sadness rises—I numb it frantically with food. Then, instead of sadness I feel fullness, which is as intolerable as sadness. So I purge it all out, and this second emptiness is better because it is an exhausted emptiness. Now I'm too tired, too wracked, too weak and worn to feel. I feel nothing but light—light-headed, light-bodied. And so bulimia becomes the place I return to again and again to be alone, to go underneath, to not feel so much, to feel it all, safely. Bulimia is the world I make for myself, since I don't know how to fit into the real world. Bulimia is my safe, deadly hiding place. Where the only one who can hurt me is me. Where I'm far away and comfortable. Where my hunger can be as big as it is, and I can stay as small as I need to.

~

There is a price to pay for sinking into bulimia, and that price is sisterhood. Until I choose bulimia, my sister and I share one life. There is nothing that is mine or hers. We even share one security blanket. I lie in bed snuggling my corner while the blanket stretches across the room to her bed, where she snuggles her corner. We sleep like that, the blanket connecting us, for years. One night she lets her side fall to the floor and I scoop it up, but she never asks for it again. She doesn't need our blanket anymore. She is less afraid than I am.

My sister's legs are long and she uses them to move through the world easily and beautifully and confidently. I can't keep up, so I build bulimia and live there. Like our security blanket, bulimia is mine and she can't have it because she doesn't need it. If there was a picture of my life's path you would see our footprints side by side and then you'd notice that one day I sat down in the sand and refused to travel any farther. You would be able tell by her footprints that she stood still for years, wondering why I was too afraid to keep walking. Wondering why one day we were together and the next we were each alone.

~

Now I'm thirteen and I'm in the front seat of my dad's truck. He's looking at the road and explaining that he and my mom found more cups in my room. Each night I bring two cups to bed with me—one filled with food and one to fill with vomit. I leave the cups underneath my bed, and their stench is a constant reminder to all of us that I'm not better. My parents' desperation is growing. They've sent me to therapy, medicated me, pleaded with me, but nothing is working. My passenger seat is pushed up farther than my dad's seat, so all of me feels huge and thrust too far forward. I feel bigger than he is, which seems like a breach. My hair is frizzed and orange and my skin is broken out so badly it's painful. I've tried to cover it with makeup, and now the brown liquid drips down my neck. I feel ashamed that my dad has to drive me around, claim me as his own. I want to be small again, small enough to be taken care of, small enough to disappear. But I am not small. I am big. I am unwieldy. I feel obnoxious and impolite for taking up so much space in this truck, this world.

My dad says, "We love you, Glennon." This is embarrassing to me, because it simply cannot be true. So I look at him and say, "I know you're lying. How can anyone love this face? Look at me!" As the words burst out, I hear them and see myself say them. I think, *Glennon. This performance is embarrassing. You're even uglier in your angst.* I wonder which voice is me—the one feeling the feelings or the one scoffing at my own feelings? I have no idea what is real. I just know that I am not beautiful, so anyone who says he loves me is saying it because it's in his contract. My dad looks shocked by my outburst and he pulls the truck over and begins talking to me. I do not remember what he says.

I survive middle school the way a whale might survive a marathon: slowly, painfully, with great effort and conspicuousness. But then, over the summer between middle school and high school, my skin clears up a bit and I find clothes that hide my barely existent heft. That summer I have an epiphany: *Maybe I've studied schools of fish long enough to pretend to belong to one. Maybe the beautiful girls will have me if I just wear the right costume, smile more, laugh right, watch the leader's cues, and show no mercy, no vulnerability. Maybe if I pretend to be confident and cool, they'll believe me.* So every morning before I walk into high school I tell myself, *Just hold your breath 'til you get home.* I throw back my shoulders, smile, and walk into the hallway like a superhero in a cape. To onlookers it appears that I've finally found myself. I haven't, of course.

What I've found is a representative of me who's just tough and trendy enough to survive high school. The magic of sending my representative is that the real me cannot be hurt. She is safe inside. So, as someone else, I have finally arrived. I hold my breath all day at school, and then when I get home I relax with pounds of food and the toilet. This rhythm works. I become popular with the girls, who sense that I know something they don't. Eventually I begin to notice the boys noticing me. As I pass them in the hallway, I practice carrying myself in a way that announces: I am available to play the game now. And then I set myself down on the chessboard and wait to be played. As pawns inevitably do, I get picked up.

~

I have one vivid memory of the first time sex happens to me: Camel Lights. One day after school, I find my sophomore self lying in my senior boyfriend's twin bed, trying to catch my breath underneath his heaviness and wondering how long sex will take. The Eagles play on his plastic boom box and the first few notes of "Hotel California" make me feel hollow and afraid. As my boyfriend squirms on top of me like a huge, frantic toddler, I scan his bedroom and see a pack of Camel Lights on the dresser. There is a green lighter lying diagonally across the pack, and for a moment the lighter and cigarettes remind me of the two of us, tossed haphazardly on top of each other, meant to be of quick and practical use to one another. I understand that I'm the lighter. Eventually he stops squirming but remains lying on top of me. "Hotel California" plays on. I wonder if the song's length is part of its message: *Life is not only eerie and hopeless but also entirely too long.* After that afternoon, he takes me to the laundry room in his parents' basement. He was just trying to make our first time special.

One hot morning in the summer after tenth grade, my best

friend and I go to the local pet store to visit the animals. My friend is considering having sex with her boyfriend and she asks me to tell her what it's like. I watch the kittens play in their cage and notice one pouncing on a nearby scratching post. I point to that kitten and say, "Sex is like that. I'm the scratching post and Joe pounces on me when he gets the urge. My body's a toy he likes to play with, but he's not all that interested in me. It's like, he's touching me—but he's not really touching *me*. Sex isn't really personal. It's just that I happen to be his girlfriend so my body is his to play with. It feels, like, childish to me. Like cats pouncing on scratching posts or kids playing with each other's toys but mostly ignoring each other. But I learned this trick: I just leave my body there to get it over with and I slip out and think about other things. I plan outfits and stuff." I turn away from the kittens and look directly at my friend. "Sex isn't something that I *have*, really, it just happens to my body while I'm up here, waiting for it to be over. But I don't think Joe knows. Or cares."

My friend stares at me silently. I can tell by her face that I've shared too much. This is not the me who is allowed to speak. This is not my representative. I wait. She says, "That's so weird. It looks like fun on TV."

"I know," I say. "It's not really like it is on TV. Not for me, at least. But, whatever, you know?" She goes back to her dogs and I go back to my kittens. I'm sixteen years old and I want my world to be small again—just kittens and dogs and my best friend.

A few weeks later, my friend has sex for the first time. She calls and says, "I don't know what you were talking about. It's the best thing in the world. It's totally amazing." I stop talking about sex after that. I just pretend, to my boyfriend and friends, that it's all totally amazing. Sex, friendship, high school, being me. *Yes, it's all totally amazing.*

~

One summer evening I watch Joe walk across a stage and accept his diploma from our high school principal. While he and his friends throw their caps in the air, I stand against the wall, thrilled to be a peripheral part of this celebration, to belong here, with them. After the ceremony, he drives me back to his house with Van Halen blasting from his car speakers. There, in the passenger seat, being driven by this graduate—looking up at the stars through his sunroof—I feel free and important and lucky and powerful. That night, at Joe's graduation party, his parents give him a present: a box of condoms. He is leaving for beach week with his buddies the next day so he'll need these, his mom says with a wink. He laughs and his family laughs, too. No one glances at me to check if I'm wondering why my boyfriend needs condoms for a trip he's taking without me. I smile. So funny. Condoms! *Boys*, you know.

Joe kisses me good-bye and heads off to beach week with his buddies and his condoms. Two days later, Rob, a boy I've known since second grade, knocks on my door. I step onto my front porch and Rob stammers a bit and then announces with a nervous smile that he needs to tell me something. He visited beach week and learned that the night before, Joe slept in jail. He was arrested because another senior girl accused him of rape. Everyone at beach week is talking about it, so Rob wants me to hear it from him before the news gets back home. He tells me that Joe was released without any charges early that morning because of "inconsistencies" in the victim's report. I thank Rob, send him home, and wait for Joe to return. I ask him about the rape and he laughs and tells me the accusation isn't true. I do not break up with him. My friends and I handle this by agreeing publicly that the girl who accused Joe of rape was drunk, stupid, jealous, and lying. I don't think that anyone actually believes she was lying, but we never admit that to each other. I don't know if this is because we just don't care or because we are adhering to the understood but never acknowledged rules that govern high school life. This one is: Disbelieve and betray other girls to remain in good standing with the popular boys. A few weeks later I run into the victim in the locker room of my mother's gym. As we pass each other, I hold my head high. She lowers hers and looks away. I feel an electric sense of defiance and victory.

Joe and I continue listening to Van Halen and drinking and laundry-room sexing for another year. When I finally break up with him, he cries while I stare at him in disbelief. I think to myself, *Why are you crying? What are you losing that's worth having?* But I say nothing. I find another boyfriend, a new basement, same parties, different brands of booze. I know how to stay underneath at night; in the light of day, hiding is harder.

~

Early in my senior year, I stand at the end of the lunch line, hold my tray steady, and look out at the sea of cafeteria tables. I try to decide how to appear aloof as I search for an empty chair. How will I make it across the slippery floor while wearing these heels? How will I keep my skintight dress from riding up, while carrying this tray? How will I cover my acne in this fluorescent light? How will I look cool while I'm sweating profusely? This is the impossible moment I arrive inside of every day. Hundreds of us have been sent to this cafeteria with two contradictory duties: Be invulnerable while doing the most vulnerable possible things—fitting in and eating. This room is like *Lord of the Flies*, and the only way to survive is to keep weakness hidden. My weaknesses are my needs: acceptance and food. These needs are entirely too human for high school. So I stand there in fear that this will be the day the real, hungry, sweaty, needy me rises too close to the surface and the sharks circle. Before I take a step forward I wish vehemently that we had assigned seats. I look out at the sea of faces and understand that we are all drowning in freedom. Where are the adults? We need them here.

I've taken too long and someone's behind me now. I pretend to spot a friend waving me over, and I send my representative toward no one. Eventually I find an available seat at a table of B-list high school celebrities. This table is not too far above or below me—a good, safe fit. I sit and try to make small talk, but it's so hard. I feel ridiculously exposed. I don't want to be beached here in public. I want to be alone and underneath. My anxiety convinces me to eat far too much for the tight dress I'm wearing. I throw away my tray and teeter out of the cafeteria and toward my relief: the bathroom stall. When I get there, I see a long line of girls. No privacy, won't work. I continue down the hall toward another bathroom. It's packed with girls fixing their makeup, laughing, gossiping, hiding. The third bathroom I find is out of order. The food I ate is settling in and it will be too late soon. I'm sweating and my heart's pounding and I watch myself take off my heels and start running through the hall. People are turning from their lockers and staring. I am making a scene. I look at them watching me and something breaks inside. Instead of looking for a fourth bathroom, I turn into the school office. The secretary asks if I have an appointment. I look at her and think, *Who has an appointment when she's this desperate? Desperation is not planned. If you only help kids with appointments, you will never help anybody who needs help.* I walk past her, open the door to the guidance counselor's office, and sit down in front of her. She looks up from her paperwork, alarmed. I say, "I'm so tired. I'm so uncomfortable. I think I'm going to die. Call my parents. I need to be hospitalized. I can't handle anything. Someone needs to help me."

I don't know what I mean. I don't know if this is a suicide threat or just a passive observation. I think I'm requesting a hospital for my body, because my suspicion is that my body is broken. But I can tell by the way the counselor looks at me that she suspects my mind is broken. She calls my parents, and that afternoon I am driven to a place for people with broken minds.

~

In the mental hospital's intake room, my family and I silently watch the nurse search my bag for anything I might use to hurt myself.

She takes my razor and my granola bar, holding each one up, smiling apologetically, then placing each inside a Ziploc bag with my name on it. My parents hold their faces steady, but I can tell their tears are right beneath the surface. My tears are there, too, but mine are tears of relief. *Yes, please,* I think, *take everything scary. Yes, yes. Keep me from hurting myself. Let me hide here. Tell me what to do, how to live. Yes. Take it, take it, take it all.*

My sister is watching, too. Her eyes are wide and she is so confused, so afraid. I can tell she is trying to be brave, but no one knows what brave looks like inside this particular moment. Does brave let me go with this woman or does brave take my hand and bust me out of here? No one knows. The nurse tells me to hug my family good-bye and I do, first my dad, then my mom, then my sister. She is trembling and I have to steel my heart so I don't crumble from the horror and shame of what I'm putting her through. I do what I have to do. I let go of her and follow the nurse down a small hallway. My family stands in the doorway, watching me go. I stop and look back at them and I feel frightened by how small they seem huddled together in the cold, white, fluorescent hallway. They stay there together and I go alone. This is how it has to be. There is them and there is me and I can't fit into their world and they cannot, should not, go with me into mine. They don't need what I need. I turn a corner and they disappear completely and now it's just me, in my world. I enter my new room and unpack again. Underneath my clothes I find a piece of paper scrawled with my baby sister's handwriting. It's the lyrics to a song.

There's a hero
If you look inside your heart
You don't have to be afraid
Of what you are

It will take me another twenty years to understand what my fourteen-year-old sister is trying to tell me. How is it that she was the only one who knew what was wrong with me and how to fix it?

When I wake up in the morning at the hospital, the only thing I have to do is brush my teeth. I don't need to shower, get dressed, or do my makeup because costumes are not required here. So I brush and then stand around in the hallway, waiting for the first bell to ring so I can line up with the other patients to get our meds. We don't make small talk in line. Everybody seems comfortable with quiet. There are no unspoken social rules we're supposed to adhere to, and as the relief of this sets in I feel my muscles relaxing, my shoulders dropping, my inhalations deepening. After we take our meds, we meet for group therapy. We sit in assigned seats around a circle and look at each other. We tell our stories. If we don't feel like smiling, we don't. Most of us don't feel like smiling. We're here because we're tired of smiling.

One day a girl with sliced-up arms says, "My mom sent me here because she says no one can believe a word I say." I look at her and I want to say: *Does she see that you tell the truth on your arms? Like I tell the truth in the toilet?* By the time we landed in the hospital, most of our families considered us insensitive liars, but we didn't start out that way. We started out as ultrasensitive truth tellers. We saw everyone around us smiling and repeating "I'm fine! I'm fine! I'm fine!" and we found ourselves unable to join them in all the pretending. We had to tell the truth, which was: "Actually, I'm not fine." But no one knew how to handle hearing that truth, so we found other ways to tell it. We used whatever else we could find—drugs, booze, food, money, our arms, other bodies. We acted out our truth instead of speaking it and everything became a godforsaken mess. But we were just trying to be honest.

My roommate's name is Mary Margaret. Mary Margaret is anorexic. Unable to speak with my little sister, I allow Mary Margaret to take her place for a while. We whisper long into the night, every night. One night, after lights out, I tell Mary Margaret about my great-grandfather. I explain that he was a coal miner in Pittston, Pennsylvania, and that every morning my great-grandmother packed a lunch pail for him and sent him down into the mines. It was dangerous work because there were deadly, invisible toxins in the mines, but the miners' bodies weren't sensitive enough to register the poison. So they carried a canary in a cage down into the mines with them sometimes. The canary's body was built to be sensitive to toxins, so the canary became their lifeguard. When the toxin levels rose too high, the canary stopped singing, and this silence was the miners' signal to flee the mine. If the miners didn't leave fast enough, the canary would die and, not much later, so would the miners.

I tell Mary Margaret that I don't think we're crazy, I think we're canaries. "Could it be," I ask, "that we aren't making any of this up—we're just sensing the very real danger in the air?" I tell Mary Margaret that I think the world is more than a little poisonous and that she and I were built to notice that. I tell her that in lots of places, canaries are appreciated. They're the shamans and the poets and the sages, but not here. I say, "We are the ones on the bow of the *Titanic* pointing and yelling 'Iceberg!' but everybody else just wants to keep dancing. They don't want to stop. They don't want to know how broken the world is, so they just decide we're broken. When we stop singing, instead of searching the air, they put us away. This place is where they keep the canaries."

I talk about canaries for a while and Mary Margaret is silent, so I assume she's sharing my epiphany. But after I finish, I look over and realize she's asleep. I climb out of my bed and walk over to her. I pull her sheets over her tiny body and kiss her forehead. She is seventy pounds and she looks like a bird who is too tired to sing. Right then I wonder if my friend is going to die soon. I wonder if dying is the only warning Mary Margaret has left for the world. I let myself hope that maybe in here we are out of the mines. Maybe in this little bare room together we are safe from the toxins.

One night, very late, Mary Margaret and I write vows promising to take care of each other forever. We both sign the vows in crayon because we aren't allowed to have pencils. Mary Margaret makes me promise not to eat the crayons. I tell her maybe she should. We laugh. Here, we feel safe enough to laugh. But when it's time to be released, we stop laughing.

~

If I could go back to the morning of my release, I would say to my parents: *I know I have to leave here—but I don't want to go back there. Not back to high school. There are too many toxins and I can't breathe.* But I say nothing. I assure everyone that I'm fine now. It's homecoming week at school and I've been nominated to the Homecoming Court and voted "Leading Leader" of my senior class. Soon after my release from the mental hospital, I sit on the edge of a convertible in a pretty blue suit, waving to crowds of people lining the sidewalks for the homecoming parade. My mother and grandmother drive me through the crowd and I can feel their hope. We've been through so much and here I am, being admired. It feels like victory to them. But I know the truth. You have to be known to be loved, and none of these waving people knows me. They only know my representative. This is not a victory parade for me, but for her. She is the one waving. I am the one holding my breath again, underneath. She is the star; I am the mental patient.

As I wave, I think about my superlative: "Leading Leader." It makes perfect sense. I am a good leader because I am a good rule follower. I understand there are two sets of rules in high school: the surface set that the adults profess and then the hidden, unspoken but understood rules that are truer and irrefutable. The hidden, truest rules about how to matter as a girl are: Be Thin. Be Pretty. Be Quiet. Be Invulnerable. Be Popular by Following the Powerful Boys' Lead. Sex and booze and eating disorders are simply ways for a high school girl to honor the hidden rules and to get from here to there. From childhood to adulthood. From invisible to relevant. There is a certain kind of life a successful girl is supposed to build, and bulimia, booze, and sex are simply the tools she needs to build it. My homecoming sash says: *You've followed the hidden rules by any means necessary. You sacrificed your health and your body and your dignity, and you looked good doing it. You did not disrupt the universe with any of your feelings or your questions. You stayed small. You did not take up too much space at all. You never surfaced, and when you needed to—when you needed oxygen—you left and breathed away from us. We never even met you. Well done.*

~

As soon as I arrive at college, I search for a school of fish in which to hide. I find it in Greek life. The game here is both new and old. The rules, of course, are: Thinness is Beauty. Beauty is Power. Power is Being Chosen by the Boys. The interesting difference between college and high school is that here the hidden rules are publicly acknowledged. Guys from a nearby fraternity occasionally hang a sign above their party room that reads: NO FAT CHICKS. Since I was ten, I've known that No Fat Chicks is the hidden rule, so it's a relief to see it made visible. Since the men have stopped hiding this rule, we women stop hiding our efforts to follow it. There are so many openly bulimic women in my sorority that there is an announcement one afternoon, "When you throw up, please flush the toilets. It looks bad when people come to the house and there's puke everywhere." As long as you flush it away, bulimia's okay. It shows dedication, adherence to the rules. *No Fat Chicks*, you know. I go home after freshman year and through a disciplined regimen of restricted eating, excessive exercise, and bulimia, I lose fifteen pounds.

I bleach my hair, buy a wardrobe full of skimpy clothes, and go back for my sophomore year, ready to play. Once again, I am picked up.

I start dating a boy from an exclusive fraternity. It is the ultimate victory to be a girl handpicked by a member of this discriminating group of boys. I have fooled everyone into believing that I am one of the beautiful ones. I follow this boy around and the frat brothers take care of me and provide me access to every secret place I want to be. I am *in* again. Every weekend hordes of women wait outside the fraternity basement in anticipation of getting to the front of the line, where a boy will look each one up and down and then check to see if her name is "on the list." Of course, her entry will never depend upon whether her name is found. It will depend upon her looks and her reputation. She needs to be hot or she needs to be easy. One of those two things is required for entry. I wonder now, *Why did we wait in that line? Why didn't we just get our own damn beer and dance in our own damn basements?*

Because of my boyfriend, I get to skip to the front of the line—past all the other less powerful, less thin, women. Access into yet another dark basement is everything, and I have it. There I can drink myself into a stupor and be carried to bed to have sex that I will not remember.

My frat boy is good and kind. Away from the matrix of campus life, we love each other. During vacations I visit his midwestern home, where we talk and laugh late into the nights. Off campus we are allowed to be human together. He writes poems for me and we plan the music that will play at our wedding—the anthem from our favorite Quentin Tarantino movie. But back on campus, there is no room for love. One evening, he leaves a tender message on my answering machine and his frat brother steals the tape. His brothers play it at a meeting with the entire fraternity present. When the men hear my boyfriend say "I love you," they collectively fall into hysterics and call him a pussy. So my frat boy learns to play his part, which is to keep me in the basement. To not be a pussy. My job is to only be a pussy. I pursue no interest in college, other than booze, boys, and getting ready to go booze with the boys.

Getting ready is my constant; it is the ritual that grounds me. The process begins around four o'clock, when I'm steady enough to get out of bed and begin drinking again. I take a beer into the shower, close my eyes, and let the water run over me, washing away the previous night's grime and sex and shame. Then I dry off and gather my tools—hair dryer, straightener, makeup, stilettos, tube top, short skirt, more beer—and begin the hard work of transforming myself from a sick mess into my shiny, beautiful, bulletproof rep. I am so proud of this process, so sure of myself here, that if I'm ready too early, I begin all over again with another shower. When I'm fully armored, I head to the basement and stay up late with the boys and sleep in with the boys and I beat them in drinking contests and out-cocaine them line for line. I am following the rules. Winning again.

Ten years later my fraternity boy will marry a woman I adore. She'll say that it took him some time to get over our relationship. She'll say that one night they were in an argument and he became distant. She'd said, "What are you thinking about?" and he'd replied, "Glennon. She just didn't give a fuck." His wife understood this to be the ultimate compliment for him to bestow upon a woman. She also understood that it was no compliment. Any woman who *doesn't give a fuck* is simply abandoning her soul to adhere to the rules. No woman on earth doesn't give a fuck—no woman is that cool—she's just hidden her fire. Likely, it's burning her up.

2

I GRADUATE FROM COLLEGE, which makes me grateful to and suspicious of my alma mater. I move back home and rent a town house with my two best friends, Dana and Christy. I get a job teaching third grade, and even though I spend the first hours of every morning sobering up, I'm a good teacher. My love for my students is my grip on the world. I lose that grip every day at dismissal when I drive out of the school parking lot and toward the grocery store to pick up two huge bottles of wine. As soon as I get home, I take a deep breath by pouring and pouring until I'm back at baseline. Until I'm numb enough. I still binge and purge, but drinking and passing out is my favorite rhythm now. Dana and Christy join me most nights, but I drink differently than they do. They drink to take the edge off; I drink to disappear. I'm almost always successful. Most nights I black out and wake up completely dependent upon Dana and Christy to fill me in on the previous night's happenings. What did I say? What did I eat? What did

I break? They always help me remember. I am their project. Eventually, I break up with my frat boy. We are each secretly worried about the other's drinking, but since quitting is inconceivable, it's not worth bringing up. Besides, the truth is that there are different rules outside of campus. I am in the real world now, so I need to be paired with a healthy, successful grown-up. These things are now more important than cool, and access to basements means nothing. As I tell him it's time for us to move on, he cries. I am single for two weeks. It is scary and strange to be a pawn in no one's hand.

The morning of July Fourth, Dana and I join the throngs of folks packing the D.C. streets in celebratory debauchery for the Independence Day Bar Crawl. Like the thousands of others here, Dana and I are people-watching, steadily sipping off our hangovers, waiting for something interesting to happen. There's nowhere to hide from the relentless sun, so we just stand still and melt. I drop my cigarette to the curb and stamp it out with my sandal. I use my free hand to shield my eyes and I scan the crowd. When I spot Craig, I hold my breath. I remember that guy. He was a year ahead of me in high school and he was untouchable—a star soccer player with all the wholesomeness and goldenness that soccer coaches require or create. After graduation, he played soccer in college and then went on to the semipros. Rumor has it that he's now a fashion model. He's so alarmingly confident and gorgeous standing there in the middle of the intersection that I feel certain this rumor is true.

I light another cigarette and study him. He's tall and solid with hair thick and black. His arms are sculpted and folded casually across his very compelling chest. I feel a strong urge to place my hand on his upper arm, to check how warm and soft his skin is, to compare the size, color, and temperature of my hand to his shoulder. He seems like he'd let me do that. His eyes are crinkly and kind. He looks comfortable in his smooth, tan skin and every time he smiles I catch myself smiling along with him. He's exotic and enticing, but in the middle of this crowd of strangers, he also reminds me of home. We grew up in the same hallways and classrooms and town. We're from the same place. I *recognize* him. He laughs at something a gorgeous woman beside him has just said, and I start to feel queasy with longing. I either need to stand next to Craig and touch him and make him laugh or never look at him again. This in-between is becoming painful.

The pain intensifies when I allow my vision to widen and realize that Craig is actually surrounded by beautiful women. Four of them have created a horseshoe around him—like he is the sun and they are each trying to warm themselves. These women are stunning. Each seems at least six feet tall, with long wavy hair pulled back from makeup-free faces. They are a toothpaste commercial. As soon as I see them, I feel oafish. What is the point of trying when women like these exist? I try to squash my longing to touch Craig's arm by collecting things to hate about these women. First of all, their legs. All eight of their legs are long and toned and their shorts are short—not in a trashy way, in a sporty way. People have no business being sporty at a bar crawl unless their sport is beer pong. Second, they are drinking not from the obligatory red plastic bar-crawl cup, but from bottles of water. *Water at a bar crawl?*

I conclude that these women are, in fact, bar-crawl imposters. It is as if they were on their way to compete in a Fourth of July beach volleyball tournament but took a wrong turn and are currently awaiting rescue by their Olympic coach or perhaps their suntan oil sponsor. I want them to go away so I can stop longing and start forgetting that people like this exist. So it's nonsensical that I nudge Dana, gesture toward Craig, and say, "Remember him?"

Dana looks over, and when her eyes land on Craig, her face brightens. She suggests we walk over to say hello. I say, "Um, no. Are you kidding? Look at him! He is too good-looking to talk to and we are too sober to do any talking. And look at those girls! No hellos. Absolutely not."

Dana says, "Craig was my neighbor. He's the nicest guy ever. And hellos are not as hard as you make them out to be."

"The hello is not the problem," I say. "The problem is after the hello. What then? Please, no. Let's stay here with our precious cups and drink safely alone. Everything is perfect. Why must you always ruin drinking by adding scary people and things?" Dana rolls her eyes and walks away. I watch her swerve through the crowd toward Craig and I become aware that I am suddenly and unacceptably alone in the middle of the crowded street. I choose the least terrifying of my limited options and follow her. Craig notices us coming. He smiles and waves us over in that way only guys who are certain they are every woman's destination know how to smile and wave women over. I am certain that every person I pass can hear my heart pounding. I sidle into their circle as close to Dana as possible. All of them tower above me. I stare at my shoes and sip my beer.

Craig is now hugging Dana, stepping closer to me. My terror alert level leaps from yellow to red. He smiles and says kindly, gently, "Hi. I remember you. Glennon, right? How have you been?" I am taken aback. I am used to men addressing me sideways and slippery, through sarcasm and innuendo. Craig's directness is alarming. To make matters more unnerving, he is looking directly at my face. Somehow it feels like he is trying to talk to the real me, not my representative. This seems like an egregious boundary violation. I stare at him for a moment and then I hear Dana say: "G? You okay?" *Yes! That's me. I am G! I remember!* But I have no idea how to answer Craig's second question: How have you been? Why would he start with such a hard one? I'd like to consider an answer but all I can think about is: *What does my face even look like in daytime conditions?* I have no idea. I am not used to caring about details, but details suddenly seem important. What is Craig actually seeing as he looks directly at me? Stray facial hair? Bloodshot eyes? Unaddressed blackheads? I don't know. I just know I did not sign up for this examination. All this light and closeness and sincere conversation feel altogether inappropriate for a bar crawl. I need to get out of here.

I hear myself say the following. "Hi. I'm fine. Great. Yes, I'm Glennon. I'm good. How are you? Dana, I have to pee." Dana looks at me and her eyes widen and she shapes her face into this question:

What the hell? I grab her hand and raise my beer toward Craig and his athletic friends in a manner that I hope translates directly to: *So long! It's been great getting to know you! I'm very busy and important and must go now! Good luck with all of your glowing and legs and, by all means, keep up the good water work! I hope all of your Olympic dreams come true!* Dragging Dana behind me, I swerve through the crowds of people, away from Craig and toward the safety of a crowded bar. I glance back and notice that Craig is watching me leave.

When Dana and I finally make it inside, I walk straight to the bartender and order two shots. I hand one to Dana, and she stares at me for a moment and then explodes into laughter. "Okay, then," she says. "That went well. You are so normal, Glennon. Really normal." She swallows her shot, slams the glass on the bar, and says, with visible confusion, "I actually think he *likes* you." This idea feels equal parts ridiculous and true to me. I tell her it must be all my charm and social grace and height and sobriety. While we laugh, I find myself wishing I'd stayed longer and tried harder with Craig. I liked standing beside him. I liked how my insides felt when he looked at me. I'd been afraid, but awake. I wanted him beside me now, being tall, confident, and good. I wanted him to put his arm around me, claim me and call me good, too. I wanted him to invite me into his toothpaste commercial. I spend the rest of the day talking to drunken, slippery, sideways guys while thinking about Craig and his goldenness and arms and kindness.

Later that night, Craig and I run into each other again, this time inside a smoky, dark, perfect bar. I'm grateful to note that Craig has graduated from both water and the Olympic girls: None is in sight. I am filled with gallons of confidence now, and as I approach Craig, I sense that the power has shifted between us. Craig turns away from the new girl he's talking to and smiles like he's been expecting me. When I get close enough, I put my hand on his arm and watch the girl walk away. I'm not nervous anymore. I might not know what to do with a golden boy during the day, but I know what the night calls for. Details like faces and answers to questions are less important now. We both have bodies, and that is quite enough to have in common. We dance, and then Craig asks if I want to go "see his place." I say yes, because his place is where we've been heading since he first smiled at me twelve hours ago. We take a taxi home and I meet a few of his buddies and then we go to his room and sleep together. I don't remember it at all. I only remember waking up late the next morning and finding myself in bed with this boy who feels both completely out of my league and just like home.

I wake before Craig, so there's time to study him up close. He looks as invincible horizontal as he did vertical. I feel nervous again. This is exactly the *after the hello* part I'd been trying to avoid. Craig opens his eyes, smiles, and wraps his arm around me. I say, "Hi," and I feel pretty solid about that effort. He smiles and says, "Hi to you." Then we silently decide that the only way to barrel through the awkwardness of being naked strangers together is to make out. We do. It feels odd and distant like sex always feels to me. Afterward, we get dressed and he drives me home. Craig calls me the next day and the day after that and we don't spend another night apart for the next four months.

~

Being with Craig feels right to me—like his goodness and light are what I've been missing. When I ask him what he likes about me he says, "You're exciting—and you aren't needy. You make me feel like all you care about is me. I feel good when I'm around you." He means this kindly, but it knocks the wind out of me. I want to say, *I know I make you feel good because I'm an expert at that. But when you look at me, do you see me as anything more than a mirror? Do you see anything here you like? I want you to notice something I'm good at other than making you feel good about yourself. What about me? Can you help me figure out who I am in here?* But I don't say any of that. I know the rules.

~

A few days before Thanksgiving, I find out I'm pregnant. There is never a question about what we will do. Craig takes me to the clinic and we sit together silently, staring at old magazines, naked strangers again. Eventually Craig looks at me sideways and whispers, "You okay?"

I nod. "Yeah. Totally. Really, I'm fine." We leave it at that. When we approach the receptionist to prepay, Craig pulls out his credit card and I wave him off. "No. I've got it," I say. I don't want to put him out. I want to be independent about this. We have not yet become comfortable splitting a restaurant bill so we are certainly not ready to split an abortion. An unsmiling nurse calls my name and I follow her into the back for the procedure. It hurts more than I expect it to.

Then Craig is ahead of me on my front porch, unlocking the door to the home I share with Dana and Christy. I follow him inside and let him lead me to the couch, where he covers me with a blanket. We sit together for a few minutes, talking about other things. He tells me that his buddy is throwing a big party that night but he's not going because he wants to stay with me. I wonder why he's mentioned this at all, but I don't ask. Instead I say, "You should go. I'm totally fine." I expect him to ignore this ridiculous suggestion.

Instead, he looks at me and says, "Are you sure?"

This is the wrong answer to the question today is asking of us. I feel my stomach clench but I smile and send my representative forward to say, "Totally. I'm fine. Go ahead. I'll call you tomorrow."

Craig brings me a glass of water, kisses me on the forehead, and walks out the door. Through the front window I watch him drive away from me, my abortion, this uncomfortable day and toward the better, easier night. I am so alone inside the quiet that my ears are ringing. I want to run to my car and follow Craig but I can't because it's bad manners to have an abortion and party plans on the same day. I am supposed to be sad, somber. So I will sit here in the quiet and do my time while Craig goes free because there is no abortion etiquette for him. And because he doesn't know that whatever just happened is something that happened to both of us. I wonder for the first time if maybe Craig isn't so golden after all.

I sit as still as possible on the couch and decide that there is nothing more intolerable than silence. Until there is. Music starts blasting from upstairs and it startles me into a sudden sweat. My heart thuds as my mind scrambles. It takes me a moment to realize that it's Christy's alarm, and then another moment to recognize Stevie Nicks's voice. Oh, my God, her voice. Her voice is worse than the silence; it's a siren, an insistence. Her voice makes my whole body ache, like she's holding me down and operating on me without anesthesia. Her voice and the music are true and deep with longing and both seem directed straight at my heart. This is not a day, or a lifetime, in which I can tolerate remembering my heart. I need to turn her off. I wrap my blanket tighter around me and start up the stairs. The blanket keeps tripping me so I give up halfway and crawl to the top. I stand back up and run to Christy's room and Stevie's voice is getting louder and closer like she's inside of me asking terrible questions. *Can I handle the seasons of my life?* I find the alarm and I yank the cord out of the wall and then there is nothing but silence again. Just like that, music to quiet. Everything to nothing with the pull of a plug. Thank God. I lie flat on my back on Christy's floor. I stare up at the ceiling and try to breathe, try to steady my heartbeat again. I hold my stomach because it's cramping badly. But it's better than the heart pain. This is better. I lie there for a minute and wonder how people can possibly listen to music sober.

Music is an invitation to feel but the quiet is an invitation to think. No thank you to both. I need a drink. I need a drink. I need the opposite of music and silence: booze. I make my way back down the stairs and into the kitchen, still clutching my cocoon of a blanket around me. I panic when I find only three empty wine bottles, but when I see the bottle of whiskey on top of the refrigerator I feel safe again. I pull a chair over and climb up, grab the bottle, descend quickly, and shuffle over to the counter. I fill my cup halfway with whiskey and the rest of the way with flat, warm, weeks-old Sprite. I've already cut this whiskey with water so frequently I'm afraid it won't work anymore, but the first swallow tastes like straight sugar and burns exactly right. The whiskey warmth starts in my mouth, travels down my throat, pools in my belly, and now my insides are also wrapped in a blanket, hushed, quieted, rocked gently to sleep. I breathe deeply and my whole body stops clenching. My hands are calm, steady now. I don't need my outside blanket anymore so I let it fall to the kitchen floor. I lean against the counter and keep pouring. I finish three drinks in five minutes and now here it comes, my favorite part, the storm after the calm. I'm starting to light up. My scared, anxious, awkward self has been put to sleep and another me has been awakened. Here she is. Here I am. Powerful, carefree, bulletproof. *Look at me,* I say to myself. *Everything was awful and I fixed it, I made it better.* I am an artist and my medium is me. I'm not afraid anymore.

I hold the whiskey in my arm like a dance partner and I smile and spin my way back to the living room, my insides warm and my outside hurting less and less. This is better, so much better, than even if Craig had stayed. I remember the second question Craig ever asked me: Want to see my place? This is my place: drunk and alone. There is no pain here at my place and there is no one to perform for but me. Every feeling is approved here and I am the music.

Two hours later, the front door opens and Christy and Dana walk inside, laughing and holding brown bags full of groceries. When they see me, they both stop laughing and stare. I am alone on the couch, curled up inside a cloud of smoke, clutching my empty whiskey bottle. I can tell by their expressions that I look worse than usual. I stare back at them and start crying because that seems like the right thing to do. I need an excuse for being this drunk, this alone, this early in the evening, so I hold my bottle toward them like I'm about to make a toast and I say: "I had an abortion today." I feel like I'm acting sad instead of feeling sad. I wonder if I look glamorously tragic, like Marilyn Monroe. I'm going for "A Candle in the Wind." I need Dana and Christy to keep wanting to rescue me. That's important here.

Dana drops her bag in the foyer, sinks into the couch, and wraps her arms around my whole body. She rests her head against my head and says: "Oh G, Oh G." Christy stands and stares at us, coat still on, bag still in her hands. She looks furious. Not at me though, never at me. These two are forever on my side. Christy says, "Where the hell is Craig? He just left you here alone?" I tell her it's not his fault, he didn't know I was upset. "I told him to go," I say.

"I don't care what you told him. It's common fucking sense," she says. "He has no common fucking sense. I am going to kill him. I am going to fucking kill him." *Okay*, I think. *Yes. This is good. Let's be mad at Craig. Just don't be mad at me. Don't be mad at me for having an abortion and don't ask me why we keep ending up here on the couch with all the booze and the tears again and again. Just sit and drink with me. Just please sit and drink with me.* They do. That's how we love each other through this day. They drop their groceries in the foyer and nobody ever puts them away. We drink together for hours—until dawn cracks open the long night. When the sun rises, Christy calls Craig and curses at him. I think he comes back and apologizes, but it's possible I dreamed that. None of us remembers for sure. Not remembering is the point.

~

After that night, I don't stop drinking often enough to maintain a life. I start missing work. My bills get forwarded to my parents. I stop calling home. My car breaks down and I abandon it in a parking lot. When the police find it, they call my parents. When my parents ask what happened, I lie. When my dad goes to retrieve my car, he looks in the glove compartment and finds DUI court papers. He comes to my work to tell me he found them. He says that when he read the papers he was so terrified and angry that he went to see a priest. He didn't ask the priest to help fix me. He asked the priest to help him survive being my father without being able to fix me. This is the most startling news I've ever heard. My dad went to see a priest? To help him accept my alcoholism? Who is going to keep trying to fix me then? I've driven my father to beg God for help. *For himself.* I am afraid because my dad is threatening to stop being afraid. He asks me to come over after work to talk.

I say, "Okay, I will." I don't go. Instead, I go out and get very, very drunk.

My phone rings the next morning and keeps ringing all day. Sometime during the late afternoon, I roll over in bed, pick it up, and say hello. It's my mom and she sounds terribly angry when she says, "Come now, Glennon. Come over right now." Her voice is insistent, scary. I stand up and look around my room and I know I should change, but I'm dizzy and I can't remember how, so I decide to go as I am. I'm still in my outfit from the night before, including four-inch stiletto heels. This is ridiculous but also convenient. I teeter into my car and chew gum to try to mask the smell of smoke and booze. I drive to my parents' house on autopilot.

They meet me at the front door and I walk into my childhood home with my head down, ashamed of what I'm wearing, ashamed of what I smell like, ashamed of my red eyes, ashamed to bring so much night and filth into this bright, clean place. I sit down on the couch and I look up at the walls covered with my school pictures. I search all my faces for clues about where it went wrong. There I am in first grade, second grade, third grade—I'm wearing pigtails and smiles, but I look sad compared to my sister's pictures, which hang right next to mine. Why was I sad? Why am I sad now? I wonder if my parents wonder the same thing when they sit here in the evenings, watching the news, wondering where I went then and where I am now. We have given up looking for a solution and now we will settle for an explanation.

The sun flowing in from the huge windows pierces into me. My head is pounding and I have to hold my hand over my eyes like a visor in the middle of the living room. My parents sit on chairs across from me looking sad, angry, and helpless. My mom's voice quivers as she and my dad ask the usual questions: Why do you keep doing this to us? Why do you keep lying? Do you even love us? I sit on the couch and I try to receive their questions, but I'm a catcher without a mitt. My face is neutral, but the part of my heart that's not spoiled is aching.

I do love them. I love them and I love my sister and I love my friends. I think I love my people more than normal people love their people. My love is so overwhelming and terrifying and uncomfortable and complicated that I need to hide from it. Life and love simply ask too much of me. Everything hurts. I don't know how people can just let it all hurt so much. I am just not up for all this hurting. I have to do whatever it takes not to feel the hurt. But what I have to do to avoid the hurt for myself hurts everyone else. My survival means I have to keep harming my people. But it is not because I don't love them, it is because I love them too much. All I can say is "I do love you," but it sounds weak, like a lie, and their faces don't soften when they hear it.

I sit and stare at my hands and I remember a story I saw on the news about a woman who had a stroke and lost all her language overnight. When she woke up, her mind functioned perfectly, but she couldn't speak. So she just lay there and tried to use her eyes to communicate her terror about being trapped inside herself. Her family couldn't translate what her eyes were saying. They thought she was brain-dead. It's like that for me, too. *I'm in here. I am good on the inside. I have things to say. I need help getting out. I do love you. My secret is that I'm good in here. I am not heart-dead.* This is a secret that no one knows but me. And now, even the people who love me the most are tired of searching for me inside here. They are giving up hope that I'm still alive. They are thinking about calling off the rescue effort. Because even if I am still alive, I am not a sympathetic case. I did not have a stroke. I've done this to myself. I've trapped myself. And maybe I'm not in there after all. Maybe this me they can see is all there is, all there ever was.

My dad is still asking questions. "Who is it that you want to be, Glennon? You know you'll never be a six-foot-four blond Barbie doll, right? Do you have a single hero in this world?" I am confused by these questions. What does a Barbie doll have to do with me? But then I look down at my fried, bleached platinum hair and my sequin tube top and padded bra and stiletto heels. *Why do I look like this? Why am I dressed like this, with hair a color not even close to my own? Why must I always try to be taller, blonder, thinner, drunker?* I don't know how to answer. I wish there was something to reveal, some horrible secret about my childhood so we would have our explanation and they could feel sorry for me. I wish someone had hurt me, so I could say, *This* is why. But I've never had an excuse for being me. So I try to answer the hero question. I whisper, "I want to be like Mom." I am humiliated by my own answer. My mother is kind, good, beautiful, honest. My wanting to be her is laughable, but none of us laughs. Because what I said was pathetic and impossible, but it was also true. It came from the inside me. So I scramble to say another true thing. I tell them about the abortion. This comes from the outside me, my representative. It's manipulation, an excuse. The abortion doesn't explain the past fifteen years of my nonlife, so I have not offered them any kind of truth really, just more pain. My parents hang their heads lower. Their shoulders sink deeper. They don't come over to me. They don't hug me and pat my head and cry with me. This is how I know my search crew is calling off the dogs.

They stand up and leave the room together and I'm left in the terrible quiet again. I sit and stare through the windows at the painted, wooden playhouse that my father built for me when I was eight. The first time I played in it, I saw a spider and never went back inside. For decades it has stood there in our backyard—empty and wasted. Looking at the playhouse now, I feel like the ache might destroy me. Why was I always too afraid to play? Why can't I appreciate anything I'm given?

My parents return and my mom says, "This is it, Glennon. If you don't stop drinking, we can't be in your life anymore. We can't stand by and watch you kill yourself or someone else. We can't continue to be destroyed by you." My mom is the good cop, so her playing the heavy is a message to me. I nod. I understand that we're in the middle of an intervention. Then my mom says they've just called the priest my dad told me about. They tell me he's expecting me, so I'm to drive straight across town to the local Catholic church. I'm always sad, but I'm rarely surprised. I'm surprised now.

God is a fresh approach to the problem of me. Other than our obligatory weekly attendance at a Catholic church, my parents haven't involved God often in our family affairs. It strikes me that if the only card we have left to play here is God, we must be desperate indeed. My parents' last effort is, quite literally, a divine intervention. "Okay," I say, "I'll go." I stand up and leave the house. I drive to the church because I know that my parents will call to make sure I've gone. I hope they will, at least. I drive to the church because it feels official that neither Craig nor my friends nor my parents are going to be able to rescue me. I have run out of places to go, so I drive toward God.

3

It's dark and I drive slowly. When I see the steeple, I turn toward it and park in the gravel parking lot underneath a streetlamp. I sit in my car for a while and try to muster up some feelings. I'll need to cry for the priest, I'm sure of that. I open the car door and climb out. I stumble through the gravel in my heels. While I'm walking, I try to smooth down my ratty hair, wipe off my smeared eyeliner, and stretch my tube top to cover my belly. I've been wearing these clothes for twenty-four hours now. I make it to the front of the church, and, as I put my hand on the big bronze door handle, I notice that I'm trembling. I haven't eaten since the day before yesterday. "We cannot watch you kill yourself any longer," my parents said. *I'm not killing myself,* I think as I open the door. *I'm just not doing what's required to live. There has to be a difference.*

I step inside the church lobby and the heavy doors close behind me. It's cold and dark. I stand still for a second, waiting. Nothing happens, and no one comes to receive me. So I look farther ahead and see another room. I walk through the glass door and step inside. In here it is red and velvety and still and warm. The incense in the air fills me and makes the space inside me and the space outside of me less empty, less lonely, less vast, more solid, more safe. I feel enveloped, as if I have stepped out of my life and into somewhere better. It's not too bright or too dark in here. The ceiling is just the right height and it makes me feel just the right size. There is enough room to feel free, but not enough to feel insignificant. I see a tray of candles flickering in front of the altar and I walk toward them, slowly, down the aisle like a bride, wobbly in my heels. When I'm halfway there, my heel catches on the rug and my ankle turns. I sit down on the floor and unbuckle all the little straps on my shoes. When I stand, holding my heels in one hand, the soles of my feet touch the red velvet carpet and the softness sends a comforting ripple all the way to the top of my head. This carpet must have been made to soothe the soles of bare feet. I keep walking and then I stop in front of the tray of lit candles. Are these wishes? Are these other people's prayers?

I look up higher and see that I am standing beneath a huge painting of Mary holding her baby. I look at Mary and she looks at me. My heart does not leap, it does not thud—it swells and beats steadily, insistently. My heart fills my whole chest but does not hurt, so I do not break eye contact with Mary. Mary is lit up bright but I am in soft, forgiving light. She is wearing a gown and her face is clear. I am wearing a tube top and my face is dirty, but she is not mad at me so I do not bother to cover myself. Mary is not what people think she is. She and I are the same. She loves me, I know it. She has been waiting for me. She is my mother. She is my mother without any fear for me. I sit in front of her and I want to stay here forever, in my bare feet, with Mary and her baby around this campfire of candle prayers. I do not know if I believe in Mary, but I believe in her right now. She is real. She is what I needed. She is the hiding place I've been looking for. My parents sent me to the right place.

While I stare at Mary, a door opens behind me. I spin around and see a priest standing there. For a moment I am afraid. I can tell he's trying not to look surprised as he takes in my clothes, my face, my bare feet. He looks surprised anyway. He smiles, but it's a tight smile. He seems tired, exasperated by me already. He says hello and asks me to follow him. I don't want to follow. I want to stay here with Mary, because she is not tired. I want to tell him it's okay, he can go, I've found what I need. But I don't say anything. I just stand up and let him lead me out of Mary's room and into a dark, narrow hallway. There is no carpet anymore and my bare feet are freezing. He stops in front of a closed door, opens it, and walks inside. I assume I am to follow him in, but first I sit down on the tiles to put my shoes back on. It takes me forever to fasten all the tiny straps. My face burns, my nausea is taking over, and I wish he'd tell me to just leave the shoes off and come inside barefoot. But he just waits and watches.

When I'm finally done, I look up and he gestures toward a chair on the opposite side of his big wooden desk. I stand up, walk to the chair, and sit down. My chair is small and plastic; his chair is large and leather. I want to ask him for a blanket to cover and warm myself, but I stay quiet. I sit in my chair and look at him and he asks me why I'm there. I tell him about the abortion and then about the drinking and the drugs because I need an excuse for the abortion. I try to tell the story sadly, try to make my voice tremble, try to sound young and lost. I feel like I just got found four minutes ago, but it seems important to be lost when I speak to this man. That is my job here, and I need to do my job so he can do his and we can be done. He sits far back in his chair, folds his hands in front of his face, and listens to me. His face does not change, not at all, the whole time I talk. The only emotion he shows is seriousness. This is all very, very serious, and it seems of utmost importance to him that I know that.

I don't like it in here. The light is harsh and fluorescent and I don't want to be lit up with all this artificial light, looking like I look, feeling like I feel. And it is not the right temperature for me in here. The priest is watching me shake and I know he's thinking that I'm some kind of junkie, and I am, but I'm also just cold. He has on long pants and long sleeves and a high collar. He's covered; my skin's exposed. I want to go back to where Mary and I were warm and lit up by the gentle, true, real, forgiving flames of people's prayers.

Just a moment ago, I was with Mary, who seemed to understand that sometimes love hurts so much that you have to cut it off with booze and food and abortions. But now I am here with this priest, God's spokesman, and he is folding his hands at me and he disapproves of all this nonsense. Moments ago, God was a mother, but now God is an administrator. I was in God's womb, but now I'm in God's office, waiting to hear my punishment. Through his folded hands, the priest starts saying strange things like: "When you see your baby in heaven, your baby will not be angry with you—he'll just be waiting patiently for you at heaven's gate. Your baby forgives you. Your baby will receive God's full acceptance because God does not hold children accountable for the sins of their parents." He delivers these facts flatly, without emotion, like he's reading me my Miranda rights, like he's delivered these lines a hundred times before. How could he possibly know these things about me and God and what happens after an abortion? And how can this man know how it feels to be young and shocked and bad and good and hard and tender, pregnant and afraid? Mary knows.

Finally it seems the priest is almost finished. He says: "You, too, can be forgiven, if first you will repent." Then he is silent.

It is clear I'm supposed to respond now. I tell him, "Okay, then. I'll repent. Where do I start? Who should I apologize to? The baby? My parents? Craig? You? Everyone?" I wonder if he knows that all I do is apologize. That's all I do. *I'm sorry, I'm so sorry, I'm sorry for being me.* My whole life is an apology, and that hasn't made a damn thing better. Mary had known. She had understood: A woman doesn't need to be told, yet again, that she's bad. She needs to be told that she's good. Mary didn't ask me to repent. She asked me to rest. But sitting in the priest's office, I see how the system works here. I have to repent to him so I can go rest with her. I do what I'm told. I apologize. "I'm so sorry," I say. "I want to be better." He nods again and then offers some magic words I'm to repeat twenty times. After I say them, I will be forgiven.

I nod and flash back twenty years. I'm at the neighborhood pool waiting in line to buy ice cream. The ice cream man is selling Popsicles for a dollar each, while a high school kid who has broken into the truck is passing out free Popsicles from the back. The ice cream man hasn't a clue what's going on behind him. I wonder if the priest knows that while he's up here charging for forgiveness, Mary's back there handing it out for free. He must not know, which is why he is insisting that God's forgiveness has a price. I am pretending to believe this and promising to pay so I can get back to Mary, who is at the back of the truck hosting a free-for-all.

The priest tells me I can go and I am flooded with relief. I want only to be back in the candlelit room where I can put my bare feet on the warm carpet and breathe in the smell of God. I keep my voice very small and tell the priest, "Thank you, thank you very much." He dismisses me in a way meant to assert his disapproval, and I am not surprised. What surprised me was Mary's approval. I need to get back to where I'm approved of. I excuse myself and I wobble back through the dark hallway, past the glass doors, down the aisle, and back to Mary. As I sit there in front of the candles, Mary, and her baby, I remember a story about churches letting homeless people sleep in their pews. I feel homeless. I wonder if the priest will let me sleep here tonight. But then I hear the door open again. It is the most painful sound I can imagine, worse than silence, worse than music. I don't turn around this time. The priest clears his throat and tells me it's time to go. He needs to lock up.

I want to cry. Instead I beg. "At night? Why do you close at night? That's when people need to come."

He says, "There are many valuable things in here."

"I know. I know there are," I tell him. But he doesn't know what I mean, so I say, "I'm sorry. I'm going." I stand up and walk out. There is no time to say good-bye to Mary and her baby.

In the lobby I see a basin full of holy water. I stop in front of it and sink both of my hands into the water, all the way up past my wrists. Then I push open the heavy doors and walk out into the cool night. I stumble back through the parking lot and into my car. As soon as I'm back in the driver's seat I stare at my hands. I lick the holy water off of my fingers so it will be inside me. Then I start my car and drive. I cry the whole way home. I do not cry because of my abortion or my parents or my alcoholism. I cry because I wanted to stay with Mary. As I cry, I realize that I am not acting sad. I am not acting. I am just sad. I feel sad, but real. Mary saw the good me trapped inside. Someone saw, and that makes me feel like the good me is real. I wish so much that the priest wasn't in charge over there. I wish I'd lit a candle for myself. I wish I'd asked Mary to remember me.

4

I STAY SOBER FOR TWO WEEKS. My sobriety strategy is to outrun my addiction, to become a moving target so my pain has nowhere to land. I stay late at work and plan extra projects for my students. I rearrange the furniture in my house and shop for far too many shoes. When I watch TV, I pace back and forth in my living room. I make it through the days by never slowing down, but as soon as the sun sets, my anxiety rises. Craig tries to help me through the nights by showing up at my house with fake beer. We sit side by side on the couch and drink, but it's as if we're trying to get somewhere without any gas. Our conversation is forced and our sex, awkward. Alcohol drove us into the same world, but now we're just living in parallel worlds. Without the alcohol we feel alone, together.

One night Craig insists that we get out and go to a party a mutual friend is hosting. It sounds like a terrible idea to me, but I tag along to avoid complete aloneness. The second we walk into the party room, I'm back in high school trying to look aloof in the midst of a low-grade panic attack. I don't know where to stand or who to stand with or what to do with my hands or how to arrange my face. People keep offering me drinks and I don't know how to respond. I watch them flitting and flirting and drinking and I feel furious with them. Why are they all laughing? What is so funny? I can't imagine what was ever so funny. And why are we all just standing around in this room? Is this what we've been doing for the past decade? Just standing around? I can't imagine what was ever so interesting about this. Still, I desperately want back in. I want back into their world, but I don't have the booze I need to get there. I stay in a corner, and when I can't handle wallowing in my awkwardness and unbelonging for another moment, I tell Craig that he needs to take me home. On the way out I stare at the vodka, whiskey, and rum bottles on the counter and I think, *There I am.* My personality, my courage, and my sense of humor are trapped inside those bottles and I can't get to them. I am not in here, I am in there. What is the point of getting sober if I don't even *like* my sober self? I start hiding bottles of vodka under my bed and take swigs before I go anywhere. I tell myself that drinking is really just part of getting ready. Booze is a tool of transformation, much like my makeup and my hair dryer. It's part of the armor my representative needs to survive out there. I will not send her out unprepared again. If life doesn't want me to drink, then life should quit being so damn scary.

Eventually, of course, I start drinking out in the open again. "I'm actually fine," I tell Craig, Christy, and Dana. "I'll limit myself to a few drinks a night." They don't say a word. They don't have to. Within a week, I'm blacking out nightly again. Each afternoon Craig and the girls tell me what I did the night before. I listen with smiles and shame. If you don't remember half of your life, does it even count? Did you really live it? I pass six more months of my life this way; half alive. Half alive is all the alive I can take.

~

One day in May, I wake up at noon, disoriented and dehydrated. I roll over and see that Craig is gone. He's left a note by the bed: "Call you tonight!" I can tell that Dana and Christy are gone, too, because the house is silent. That's the difference between us; we all drink, but Craig and the girls do other things, too. Not me. I drink and I recover from drinking. Alternating between those requires my whole self. I put my feet on the floor, pull on sweatpants and a hoodie, and wrap my blanket tight around me. I slowly make it down the stairs, grab a water bottle and a jar of peanut butter, and sit down in front of the TV. As soon as I get comfortable, I catch a whiff of the full ashtray on the coffee table and a wave of nausea carries me to the bathroom. Now I'm on the floor, arms around the toilet. I just have to get it all out and I'll be fine. My body is racked, and between bouts of puking I rest my cheek on the cool toilet seat. When I think I'm finished, I make my way to the couch, using the wall and the edges of our other furniture to steady myself. The nausea doesn't stop. Two hours later, I'm still sitting on the floor, leaning over the toilet. It occurs to me that last night my breasts looked extra full in my tight top. I cup my hand underneath one of them and lift. Too much volume, I think, too heavy, too tender. *Shit. Shit, shit, shit.* I rest my cheek on the seat again.

By five, I'm stable enough to drive to the drugstore. I walk over to the pharmacy, choose the cheapest pregnancy test, and grab a bottle of pills for my pounding headache. I place both in front of the cashier and keep my head down. When I get home I go straight to the bathroom to pee on the stick. Then I place the test on the counter next to the sink and sit down on the floor to wait. I feel the chill of the bathroom tiles on the back of my thighs and the solidity of the wall against my back. I sit there until I'm certain that three minutes have passed. I don't want to stand again so I pull myself up a bit on the edge of the sink and reach blindly until I can wrap my fingers around the test and pull it down into my lap. My eyes are closed. More than anything, I don't want to have to open them. I open them. There is a small blue cross in the window. I pick up the instructions sitting next to me and read them to confirm that the cross means yes. Yes, you're pregnant. *I'm pregnant.*

At first I only feel overwhelming thirst. I use the wall to help me slowly stand up, and since there's no glass, I lean over, cup my hands under the running faucet, and carry handful after handful of water to my mouth. Water splashes all over my face and down my hoodie and soon I'm soaking wet. I sit back down and stare at the little blue cross. What happens next does not feel like a decision, but a discovery.

I become aware, there on the floor, that I will have this baby. I am hit with a wave of shame at this decision—more shame, even, than I had ending my last pregnancy. I look down and see my shaking hands, my dirty pants, the filthy bathroom floor. I am a drunk. I am a bulimic. I cannot love a child, because all I do is hurt the people I love. I cannot teach someone else how to live because I am only half alive. There is no one on earth, including me, who'd consider me worthy of motherhood. And yet. As I stare at that little blue cross, it is impossible for me to deny that someone decided I was worthy. Someone, something, sent this invitation. So many things are true at once: I am empty, alone, addicted—and still, invited. I wonder who this persistent inviter is. I think of Mary and her baby and her approval of me. I think of how she invited me toward her just as I was. I think about how she passed out forgiveness and worthiness like grace was a free-for-all. And I get stuck on that phrase as it runs through my mind. *Free for all.* Maybe grace is free. Free for the taking. Maybe it's even free for me. This free-for-all overwhelms me, fills me, covers me, convinces me. I decide to believe. Something in me says yes to the idea that there is a God and that this God is trying to speak to me, trying to love me, trying to invite me back to life. I decide to believe in a God who believes in a girl like me.

The God I decide to believe in is the God of the bathroom floor. A God of scandalously low expectations. A God who smiles down at a drunk on the floor, wasted and afraid, and says, *There you are. I've been waiting. Are you ready to make something beautiful with me?* I look at the blue cross and decide I will let it be. I will stop deeming myself unworthy of invitations and trust the inviter. I will test out the ridiculous, nonsensical possibility that somehow, in some way I can't yet see, I will rise to meet this call.

Yes, my soul says, *even though all I see is evidence to the contrary, I will believe I am worthy.* I brace myself in case there's a response. *Yes,* I say, once more, *thank you. Consider this my RSVP. Plus one. I would like to come back to life now, please. I would like to become a mother. What now?*

I look up at the ceiling, hoping to see God, but I only see brown stains from a water leak. I close my eyes and remember Mary. She is holding her baby boy and she is smiling and her eyes insist that no one is angry with me, they've just been waiting for a yes. It's time to begin, she is saying. *But I am afraid and confused and young and single and pregnant.* So am I, Mary says. And then, as I sit on the floor, I remember that today is Mother's Day. *This is the day. Let it be.*

I feel warmth and a perfect peace until the next truth surfaces as slowly and solidly as the little blue cross had: Having this baby will mean getting sober. Oh, my God. This is the difference between God and booze. God requires something of us. The booze numbs the pain but God insists on nothing short of healing. God deals only with truth and the truth will set you free, but it will hurt so badly first. Sobering up will be like walking toward my own crucifixion. That's what it will take, though. That's what it will take to rise.

I reach up, open the bathroom door, and crawl out into the hallway. I need to get to my phone. I feel afraid out here, because the hallway is big and empty and I need to be held. I stand up, run to my room, grab my phone, and carry it back to the tiny bathroom. I lock the door, sit back down on the tiles, and prop myself up against the wall again. I am still holding the test. I will not let it go. It is my proof that I'm invited. I call my sister. She answers on the second ring. "I need help, Sister. I need to get better. I don't know what to do."

"Where are you?" she says.

"On my bathroom floor."

"Stay still. I'll be there in a half hour."

On the path of our lives, this is where my sister's footsteps rejoin mine. She was miles and miles ahead of me, but the moment she heard the words she'd been waiting to hear—the moment she heard *I need help*—she turned around and doubled back. She ran as fast as she could, sand flying, tears streaming, returning to the exact place I'd sunk to the sand nearly twenty years before. When she reached me, she leaned over, grabbed my hand, and helped me stand. My legs were wobbly so she held on tight. She never asked for an explanation or an apology. She just said, *I'm here*.

~

We pull up to a church in a part of town I've never been. We climb the front stairs, open the doors, walk past the church offices, past the sanctuary, and down into the basement where the meeting's being held. I open another door and sit down in a circle with the first group of honest people I've met since leaving the mental hospital. They look tired and banged up, but real. There are no representatives in this circle. When the meeting begins, there is a language spoken that I recognize as truth. I say nothing and that's okay. There is no social normalcy I am responsible for maintaining. The jig is up for us, thank God. These are the folks who are ready to quit pretending and begin again. I feel safe with them. On the way home from the meeting I tell my sister I'm going to drive to Craig's and tell him about the baby. She asks if she can take me, and I say, "No, this part I need to do alone. It's time for me to quit pretending and begin again."

Later, I sit on the edge of Craig's bed, listening to him frantically list our "options." I hear myself say, "The thing is that I am having this baby no matter how you feel about it." I think: That's the first time I've said *this is what I want, so this is what I'm going to do* instead of *What do you want? What do you want me to do?* This shift has thrown Craig off, and he's grabbing the wall for support. I am unable to help him through this landslide moment because it's taking all of me to steady myself. But steady, I am. Craig is staring at me like he's never met me before. He hasn't. I am new. All the rules have changed for me. How this man feels about me is no longer my greatest concern.

So we sit, side by side, strangers again, with some unknown being we accidentally made between us, each of us utterly alone and never alone again. I have decided that I'm ready to stop destroying myself and start creating. I have already accepted my invitation and no one will convince me again that I'm not worthy. Not ever again. I have been invited and I have said Yes. My Yes is final. From now on, when I sense *No*—in a facial expression, in a tone of voice, in someone's disapproval of me, in my own mind—my mental response will be, *Fuck you. Fuck you* is what I say to fear, to doubt, to shame, to every form of *No, Glennon, not for you*. Fuck you is all the language I have for now. It's my shield. It's my ode to Mary. It's my prayer and my battle cry.

The next night, Craig and I sit with my parents and I tell them about the baby. They are, at the same time, weary and ready for battle. My mother looks past Craig, directly at me, and says: "You do not have to marry him, Glennon. We can raise this baby together. We can do this." This is the bravest thing anyone has ever said to me. The rest of the conversation is very hard. My parents ask us questions we are not ready to answer. Where will you live? Will you get married? We don't know. We can't even look at each other when my parents ask these questions. It's humiliating to acknowledge how much we don't know.

On the way home from my parents' house, Craig dresses his panic in enthusiasm. He says, "I know what we can do! What if you get an apartment and I get an apartment and I come stay with you and the baby on the weekends?" He is trying to hold on to his old life and have his new life, too. I understand, but it won't work. I don't need him that much. Or I need him more than that. I say, "That could work, if we break up first. We need to move forward together or move forward separately, but I'm not going to live in the in-between. You need to decide, and I don't want guilt to affect your decision. You heard my family. They will help me. The baby and I will be fine." We stop at a red light and Craig turns toward me. He does not look relieved, he looks hurt. I am confused by his hurt. I'm just trying not to be needy. Does he want us to need him or not? I don't know. He doesn't know.

We decide to take some time apart. He drops me off at home and I climb the stairs and go to sleep. On my way out to my car the next morning, I see an index card taped to my front door. It says, "Everything will be okay." It's written in my dad's handwriting. He must have driven over in the middle of the night to leave this message for me. I believe him.

I do not take my sobriety one day at a time, because every day is an eternity. I tell myself that I will do only the next right thing, one thing at a time. I start to think of my life as a path. I can only count on the next step to appear once I've committed to the step right before it. I wake up every day and ask myself: What would a sober, normal, grown-up person do next? She would get up and make her bed. She would eat breakfast. She would drink a glass of water. She would shower, then go to work. So I do these things, one thing at a time. And since I am doing the right things, I expect life to start being wonderful. I am horrified to learn that sobriety is, in fact, horrible. The first two weeks I shake and itch and feel desperate for a way to escape myself. I am claustrophobic in my own skin. Everything hurts. My beloved numbness is gone and I'm reminded, every moment, why I started drinking in the first place. But I do not drink. I do not binge and purge. Instead, I read books about babies. I keep my pregnancy test by my bed and I pick it up to check the blue cross several times a day, just to be certain. Just to remind myself that my invitation is real.

One night, several weeks into my sobriety, I lie down on my bed and my eyes wander to a pile of CDs in the corner of my bedroom. I stand up, walk over to them, and shuffle through the pile until I find the Indigo Girls. I hold them in my hand and wonder if I dare to let them sing to me. I open the case, slide the silver disc into the player, and press "play." Then I lie back down and wait for the music to hurt too much. When they start singing, I begin to feel that familiar ache that music always brings. I hold my breath, but I quickly realize that my ache feels different than it used to. Music usually makes me feel left out and yearning, like I'm looking at a photograph of a party I wasn't invited to. But now I feel drawn in, pulled closer, like the music is a bridge between these two women and me. I feel comforted. The Indigo Girls promise me that it's okay to feel too much and know too little. They insist that my sadness is not new, it's ancient. I listen for hours and every song makes me feel less alone and more a part of a universal, underground sisterhood. Gradually, I feel something like joy growing inside of me. This joy brings me to my feet and I start to dance. I dance in my bedroom, all by myself, with Amy and Emily. No one is watching me, which means I'm not performing. I'm just dancing. Whirling, whirling. For me.

This becomes my ritual. Instead of drinking, every night I shut my bedroom door and meet with the Indigo Girls. Sometimes I whirl, but usually I just lie in bed and practice feeling my feelings.

The music is a safe place to practice being human. In the span of one song I can feel it all, let it all come—joy and hope and terror and rage and love—and then let it pass. The song always ends. I survive every time. This is how I know I'm getting better: I become able to survive the beauty of music. I have accepted another one of life's dangerous invitations: the invitation to feel.

My heart seems to be doing its job, so I wonder what my body is capable of. As I listen, I hold my hands over my growing belly. I feel my thighs expanding, my breasts swelling, and my cheeks filling in. I feel grateful for all of it. For the first time in my life, I want to be big. I want to keep growing large enough to hold my baby. Some nights, as I lie there in bed growing and practicing being human, I wonder what Craig is doing. Is he out partying? Or is he in bed, too, wondering how to respond to his invitation?

Eventually Craig calls and asks me to dinner. When he comes to pick me up, I'm waiting for him by the window. As I watch him climb out of his truck, my body floods with affection and relief. I can do this alone, but I don't want to. I want the dream. I want to be a family. After dinner, he drives me to his parents' house and we walk to the backyard. He leads me past the koi pond to a swing that sits beneath a white gazebo. I sit down on the swing as Craig falls to one knee, holding a diamond ring up toward me. He is shaking when he says, "Will you marry me?" For a moment I wonder if he's afraid that I'll say no or afraid that I'll say yes. I say yes. Craig's face breaks out into a smile as he slides the ring on my finger and rises to sit next to me on the swing. He holds my hand in his and we stare at the ring together. He tells me that he got the money for it by emptying a bank account he opened when he was in middle school. When he was twelve, he started mowing lawns for his father and then expanded his business to the whole neighborhood. He made twenty bucks a month and he put it all away, saving it for something important. He says, "I was just a kid. I didn't even know that I was mowing lawns for you and our baby." I look at him and love him. We go inside to show Craig's mom. She takes my hand in hers and tells me that the ring is beautiful and that I am, too. She hugs us and claps her hands. I drive to my parents' house and it's late so I unlock the door, climb the stairs, and wake them up. I sit on the edge of their bed and hold my hand out for them to see. They look at my eyes before they look at the ring. Both my eyes and the ring are clear and sparkly—full of promise. There will be a wedding day. I am going to be new. I am ready to put who I was behind me. Shove it all into a box and tuck it away. Together, we are beginning again.

5

I'M BACK IN Craig's childhood backyard. My father and I stand side by side at the edge of a long white carpet, waiting for the right music to start so we can begin our walk toward Craig. My heels are so high that my shoulders are almost even with my father's. I'm wearing fake eyelashes and a rhinestone tiara in my hair. My hope is that they will distract everyone from my bulging belly.

My dad takes my hand, turns to me, and says, "You look exactly how I always imagined you'd look at this moment." I do not know how to respond because this moment is nothing I've ever imagined. I smile and squeeze his hand back. Our music begins and now he is walking me down the carpet, past my grandmother and my mother, past Dana and Christy, past Craig's aunts and uncles and mine. When we reach the end of the carpet, I hear the minister say, "Who presents this woman to be married?" My father says, "Her mother and I do." I look back at my mom and she is so beautiful, so young. She is wearing a bright red dress like my sister's, and she is concentrating—her whole body at attention out of love for me. She is protecting me and vouching for me, even if in this moment she can only do it with her posture. She is sitting next to her best friend, her mother, my grandmother, Alice. They are holding hands. I hope that somehow they're having the shared moment they imagined.

My father passes my hand to Craig. There is no time for my hand to be in no one else's hand. There is just not enough time. Craig takes my hand and suddenly we are alone, facing each other. This feels too intense, so I turn away from Craig and toward the minister, even though I know it's too early for that. Craig watches me and then he turns, too. I look sideways at Craig's face and I'm surprised by how young he seems, like a child playing dress-up in his father's tuxedo. I wonder if Craig is thinking the same about me in my strapless dress, eyelashes, and rhinestones. This possibility brings a wave of embarrassment and again I break eye contact. I notice that his hands are shaking. He is afraid. I am suddenly a pool of tenderness for all of us: Craig, me, my dad, my sister and mother and grandmother and the minister. We might not be ready, but we are here. We have all shown up for each other.

While the minister looks for his notes, I glance over my shoulder at our families sitting silently in the white benches that Craig's father has collected and painted just for today. They smile at me with faces full of naked hope and fear. I smile back and my breath catches. Something about the mixture of their hope, fear, and fancy shoes strikes me as tragic. I can no longer remember the difference between hope and fear. I cannot tell if anyone is happy. Is this a happy occasion? Are we happy? I feel confused and then ashamed because confused is not something a bride is supposed to be on her wedding day. Nervous seems appropriate, though, so I stay there. I'm nervous that I am unable to make eye contact with anyone at my own wedding. I turn my back toward the minister again. I lift my chin and feel my spine straighten. The sun meets my face and I imagine that its rays are holding me up. I don't know what to do with my hands so I clasp them together underneath my belly and I hold my own hands.

I am no longer a pool of tenderness. I am a tree. Everyone else can be hopeful and afraid but I am neither. I am resolute, solid, and separate. The world for which I am responsible is inside of me now. I can only save this baby who came and trusted me to come back to life. I cannot be distracted by anyone else's feelings. I will be fierce and steady, like my mother.

When it's time for our vows, I tell Craig that he is my proof that God knows me, trusts me, and loves me. I know I'm actually talking about our baby. Our baby is my proof. I don't know what Craig is to me yet. Craig accepts my vows and then begins his. He's memorized them, which seems promising. He vows to put me before all others for the rest of his life, and I look into his eyes and accept his promise on behalf of our baby. He can't be making these promises to me, because we don't know who I am yet. I have been my sober self for only four months. Maybe this is why everyone looks so afraid and hopeful. I hear the minister say my new name, Mrs. Melton. I decide that it's just as well that no one knew me before, because now I'm a brand-new person. I am no longer Glennon Doyle. I'm Mrs. Melton.

The ceremony is over and U2's "Beautiful Day" is playing and we are taking pictures. The whole wedding is now being transported from Craig's backyard to my parents' house, six houses away. We are dancing in my parents' living room to our song, which Craig has chosen. The chorus repeats, *You think I'd leave your side, baby? You know me better than that.* I wonder if through these lyrics Craig is telling me that he is saving me instead of choosing me. Or if maybe this song is for our baby, too. Maybe our romantic wedding song is actually a lullaby.

We wave good-bye to our parents and drive to a fancy hotel in Washington, D.C., for our twelve-hour honeymoon. When the man at the front desk congratulates us I feel embarrassed, like all three of us know that Craig and I are just pretending to be newlyweds. Our room is lovely but we're not sure what to do with ourselves there, so I excuse myself to change. I try on three pairs of pants before one of them successfully slides over my belly. Our baby is with us on our wedding night and this makes me feel safe, like the two of us aren't on our own. Our baby is our buffer, our shield, our reason. We go to dinner and try to talk about things important enough for a day like today. We're not very good at conversation, so we just hold hands and walk the D.C. sidewalks. I try to think about *us* and *our future* but mostly I think about how terribly hard it is to celebrate anything without booze. We head back to the hotel early and snuggle under the covers. I'm wearing the maternity wedding night lingerie my aunt sent me, which is so odd I can't think about it directly.

As Craig starts kissing me, I feel nervous and reverential because now—since there is paperwork, sobriety, a ring involved—sex will be different. It will be holy and meaningful. I am about to understand what all the fuss is about. But as Craig climbs on top of me, I find myself scanning the room to distract myself, just like I did the first time and just as I've done every time since. Then, on cue, I close my eyes and slip out of my body. When it's over, I feel afraid. It was supposed to be different, and it wasn't different. To arrive inside the moment in which you are supposed to feel more connected than at any other moment of your life and still feel lonely is utterly terrifying. It is the most lonely you can possibly feel.

I turn away from Craig and hug my belly. Craig wraps his arms around me from behind and tells me he loves me. I say, "I love you, too." We are both telling the truth. We do love each other. That's what we are supposed to do. Soon I hear Craig's breathing change. He is asleep. I'm wide awake and alone. I have just gotten married. I have just had wedding night sex. I am lying next to a man who loves me while his baby grows inside of me. If I am still lonely now, then that is it. I will always be lonely. What if marriage is not a fresh start at all? What if marriage is just a continuing? I'm afraid that today I did not turn into something new after all. What if we didn't become?

It will be okay, I silently tell all three of us. *Maybe becoming happens slowly. We will grow into all of this somehow.*

PART TWO

6

We do grow. We grow into a lot of things. Craig and I rent an apartment and I learn domesticity by paying close attention to commercials featuring wives. I follow one TV wife's lead and buy ten bottles of chicken marinade. Every afternoon I call Craig at work to make my dinner announcement: Tandoori chicken tonight! Southwest Chipotle chicken tomorrow! Never does Craig ask if we will ever eat anything other than marinated chicken. Never do I consider the possibility that there are other dinner options. I pack Craig's lunch for work and tuck inside string cheeses, juice boxes, and love notes from me and the baby. Never does Craig ask why I pack his lunch like he's in kindergarten. Never do I consider that the TV moms are packing these lunches for their children, not their husbands. Every morning Craig gets dressed up in his suit and tie, kisses me good-bye, and grabs his paper bag lunch covered with Magic Marker hearts from the counter. We walk out to his truck together and he climbs in and kisses me good-bye. I watch and wave until his truck turns a corner and disappears. I am so proud of us. We are grown-ups.

We spend our weekends decorating our apartment. We paint one living room wall royal blue. We call it our "accent wall" and feel cultured about it. We spend an entire day at a pet store choosing an aquarium and seven fish, all of which we name. We set up the aquarium in front of our accent wall and the silver fish flash back and forth against the deep blue. When we have visitors, we bring them here first. "This is our accent wall and these are our fish!" On these tours, we always save the nursery for last. As we slowly open the door, we expect everyone to gasp like we do.

The baby's room makes me want to whisper and tiptoe. Craig's mom sews us teddy bear curtains, which filter the window light so that it falls onto the crib like a gentle spotlight. Every time I walk in, I obey the spotlight and pause to stare at the crib. I take in the pastel blankets, plush-stuffed lamb, and teddy bear sheets that match the curtains and I think, *Yes, this crib is where the baby of a good mother would sleep.* Every evening when I get home from teaching, I spend hours on the floor of the nursery. I sit in front of piles of baby pajamas, unfolding them, holding them up to the light, pressing them against my face, inhaling deeply, restacking them into neat piles, and then tucking them into the dresser that Craig has painted baby blue.

One afternoon I realize that I have failed to consider this room from the baby's perspective. I go to the kitchen for a step stool, place it in front of the crib, and climb over and inside. As my foot hits the tiny mattress, the crib creaks loudly but manages to hold me.

I curl up in the fetal position with my cheek on the sheet and I look around the room with a critical eye. I am pleased by the smell of the sheets, but I decide to rearrange the shelf of toys so that more of the brightly colored ones are at the baby's eye level. I have a very, very difficult time getting out of the crib. I lean too hard on the side and something snaps. I have broken my baby's bed. I start to cry. Craig hears the crack and the crying and he appears at the door. He freezes for a moment as he tries to understand why his very pregnant wife is hanging precariously over the railing of the crib. He runs to my side and carries me to the floor. We stare at each other for a moment and then I say, "I read that we need to try to see the room from the baby's point of view." I did not read this, but I feel confident that someone somewhere must have written it, which makes it true-ish enough. I watch Craig's face. He's deciding if he should ask further questions. He says, "You're such a good mom already. I'll fix the crib, no problem. So how does everything look from there?"

Craig holds my hand as I lie on the examination table and stare at a computer screen, trying to make sense of our ultrasound pictures. First, the technician says: "Well, it's a boy."

I look at Craig and he says, "It's a boy? So it's a real *person?*" I laugh. I cannot believe it. I cannot believe any of this. I want to cheer, but my excitement is tempered by our technician's seriousness. She's distant and at first I feel angry—*What the hell's wrong with her? No trumpets? Can't she see a prince has been announced?*

But as I look more closely at her face, I start to feel afraid. She's stoic and silent and she won't allow her eyes to meet mine. She finishes her part, tells us to wait for the doctor, and leaves the dark room. Craig and I do not speak.

The doctor walks in and quickly tells us that our baby has a cyst on his brain, a bright spot on his heart, and a thick neck. He says that these are markers for "a certain chromosomal issue." His face is grim and stern, like he's mad at us about this. I don't know what issue he's referring to, so I understand that my baby is going to die and it is my fault. This makes horrible, perfect sense to me. *You do not get to spend your life as a drunk and have an abortion and then have a healthy baby and sit on the floor smelling pajamas and being happy. This is what happens. Your baby dies.* I am getting what I deserve. I am embarrassed that I ever thought I could get away with all of this happiness. There is no starting over, there is only continuing on.

I hear myself say, "Is my baby going to die?"

"No," the doctor says. "But it's likely that he has Down syndrome." I can breathe again. My baby is going to live. I close my eyes.

Craig asks, "Honey, are you okay?"

"Yes," I say. "Just give me a second." I am trying to imagine what a little boy with Down syndrome who is part me and part Craig might look like. I am trying to see my son. An image of a two-year-old materializes like a gift. He has slanted almond eyes, olive skin, and thunderous thighs. He is laughing and running away from me but I am gaining on him and I scoop him up and bury my nose deep into his neck. We both giggle madly. We are beautiful. This understanding wraps around me like a blanket.

I open my eyes. I am smiling but the doctor is still scowling. I feel a deep dislike for him. I want him to stop pretending that he's in charge of how we feel about this. I want him to stop thinking he has delivered bad news simply because he's discovered part of who my son is. My son will be who he is. I *want* my son to be who he is. I meet Craig's eyes and there is fear there, but also relief and a glint that suggests he is ready to kill this doctor. Craig leans down and whispers, "Let's get our guy out of here." *Yes,* I think. *Let's.* I tell the doctor I'd like to get dressed and he says something about further tests and we say thank you and good-bye.

We stop at a library on our way home. There is an aisle filled with books about special needs and we find several about Down syndrome. We take a stack of books, sit on the floor together, and read for an hour. This aisle, the special needs aisle, is where we have landed. We learn that the test the doctor referred to is called an amniocentesis and that one in every few hundred accidentally ends the pregnancy. I sit and think about this for a minute. Another image enters my mind, this one of a roller coaster with a sign at the entrance that reads: WARNING: ONE OF EVERY FEW HUNDRED RIDES ENDS THE PASSENGER. I tell Craig about the roller-coaster sign and we agree quickly that we will not let our boy, who we've already named Chase, ride that roller coaster. There will be no further tests. I say to Craig, "We just made a decision for Chase. We are being parents together. We are parenting."

Craig says, "This is the weirdest, scariest, coolest day of my life."

For a long while, we sit shoulder to shoulder, our backs against a shelf of parenting books, silently staring at nothing together. Something is settling in. Something happened to us in that exam room. We have gotten all tangled up with each other.

We begin to understand that to coparent is to one day look up and notice that you are on a roller coaster with another human being. You are in the same car, strapped down side by side and you can never, ever get off. There will never be another moment in your lives when your hearts don't rise and fall together, when your minds don't race and panic together, when your stomachs don't churn in tandem, when you stop seeing huge hills emerge in the distance and simultaneously grab the side of the car and hold on tight. No one except for the one strapped down beside you will ever understand the particular thrills and terrors of your ride.

We put the books back because we don't have a library card. Having a baby is one thing, but applying for a library card is another thing entirely. As we walk out into the sun, Craig says, "Is it going to be okay? He's going to be okay, right?" I look at him and understand that when your coaster partner gets scared you must quickly hide your own fear. You can't panic at the same time. You must take turns. I grab Craig's arm, hold tight, and say, "Yes. Absolutely. It's all going to be okay. He is going to be amazing. This is just part of our ride." I am smiling. Not because I am not afraid, but because I am deeply, solidly, unshakably happy.

~

I gain sixty pounds because the baby loves chocolate chip cookies and rocky road ice cream, and providing for him daily is very important to me. I am only five foot two so I begin to resemble a cube. I am mostly an ecstatic cube but every so often I wonder if instead of healing from my bulimia I have become a half-bulimic—all bingeing, no purging. Craig tells me I look fantastic every day. He says, "You're glowing!" He buys a machine that looks like a CB radio and he presses it to my belly after dinner and reads children's stories into it. Then we lie together on the couch, spooning and watching TV. During the commercials Craig touches my stomach and says again and again: "I can't believe there's a boy in there. We made a *person*. I can't believe it." I can't believe it either, but it proves to be true.

One snowy January evening, Craig and I are lying next to each other in bed and the contractions begin. I squeeze Craig's arm hard and widen my eyes. He springs out of bed and starts using the breathing techniques we learned in birthing class. Craig wants to hurry me into the car, but I insist on showering, drying my hair, and applying makeup. My baby is about to meet his mama for the first time, and I want him to think I'm beautiful. We finally get into the car and begin driving. Craig is visibly terrified. Without taking his eyes off the road he keeps saying: "We're almost there, honey. We're almost at the airport." The contraction pain has rendered me unable to speak, so I silently pray that Craig is not actually taking us to the airport. By the time we tumble into the hospital waiting room I'm screaming and Craig continues to be the only one using breathing techniques. A nurse rushes over to the big glass doors to meet us and she seems alarmed by my appearance. She looks at Craig and asks, "How long has she been like this?"

Craig says, "Nine months." At first I'm sure that he's misunderstood the question but then I think maybe not. We are wheeled into the delivery room fast. Comforted by all the beeping, machinery, and scrubs, Craig becomes the perfect partner, rubbing my legs, kissing my forehead, and remaining calm—until they turn me around to administer the epidural. I close my eyes, squeeze Craig's sweaty hands, and hear him say the following: "Oh my God! That is the biggest needle I have ever seen in my life!" There is silence and I open my eyes in time to see the nurse look directly at him, shake her head in disbelief, and mouth the word: WOW. I look up at Craig and say out loud, "Yes, honey. Wow."

While the blessed epidural does its job, my parents and sister burst into the delivery room. We squeal and squeeze each other mightily. I ask them to look in my bag for the letters I've written to thank them for believing in me. The letters are promises that believing in me was the right thing to do this time. My sister and dad find the letters and start to walk to the waiting room together. My mom lingers and takes my hand. I can tell she is trying to transfer every ounce of her hope and strength out through her arm and into me. Her eyes are full and her lip is quivering and she whispers, "God bless you, sweetheart."

This is the first time she's ever said these words to me. I feel thrilled and scared. Then she is gone and I am staring at Craig and I'm pushing and pushing and there he is: Chase Doyle Melton. I see his back before the nurse whisks him away. He looks purple and he's silent. My heart stops. I ask, "Why isn't he crying?" When no one answers I understand that this is when I get punished. This is it. "*Why the hell isn't he crying?*" I yell. Chase starts to cry.

"He's fine, honey," Craig says. "He's fine. He's perfect." Craig is crying, too. We are all crying now. The nurse hands Chase to me wrapped up in a blanket. The moment I hold him is one of the first in my life I do not feel like I am acting. His body fills my arms and I think, *Oh. So this is what my arms are for.* In that instant, I forget my loneliness. I am this baby's mother. He is mine. I am his. He is the key I've been waiting for my entire life. I am unlocked. Chase and I belong to each other.

A few hours after Chase is born, a doctor I don't recognize comes to examine him. I hand Chase over reluctantly and watch the doctor's face carefully. After several minutes he hands Chase back to me and says, "Your son is perfectly healthy. Congratulations, Mom."

He turns to walk away and I call after him, "Just one question: Does Chase have Down syndrome?"

The doctor looks back, raises his eyebrow, and says, "No. I usually lead with that." I look down at Chase and at first I feel the loss of who I thought he was and then I am filled with joy for who I know he is now. He has always been this baby boy. He is the boy with almond eyes and thunderous thighs, laughing and running. This is my son. During my decades of addiction I'd quit believing that I deserved to be a mother. I have only been a grown-up for eight months, but I am Chase's mother, and as I look at his pink lips I think, *I am no longer half alive. I am fully alive. You, baby boy, have brought me into the world.*

Two mornings later, the nurse peeks into our hospital room and sings, "Time to go home, Meltons." My first thought is that she has made a mistake. There are no doctors or machines or fancy thermometers at home. Home is no place for a child. Craig grabs my hand and says, "You and me, honey. We've got this." It's clear that he has practiced these lines, and I'm touched. I dress Chase in his going-home outfit and then shuffle slowly to the bathroom to get myself ready for my new life. I pull my sassiest prepregnancy jeans out of my bag and realize with confusion that I cannot pull them past my calves. *But I had the baby two days ago,* I think. *Maybe it takes a whole week.* I pull my maternity pants back on, walk out of the bathroom, and lie, "Okay, I'm ready."

The nurse wheels Chase and me toward the exit while Craig follows behind with our bags. Cold air blasts us as soon as the automatic doors part, so Craig hurries us to the car. I quickly buckle Chase in his seat and climb in next to him while Craig settles into the driver's seat. Neither of us speaks until we are halfway home. We cannot believe how much the world has changed during our short stay in the hospital. Apparently, our city has exploded with swarming people, jarring horns, and trucks releasing clouds of deadly gases into the sky. The oncoming traffic is a relentless procession of metal death missiles inches from obliterating our little family. We are a tiny, silent army in a tank trying to make progress through hostile territory. *My God,* I think. *We will definitely have to stop driving.* I look at Craig's hands on the wheel and his knuckles are white. I say, "Have there always been so many cars?"

He says, "I don't know, but I hate them all. Let's just be silent and concentrate." For the remainder of the trip, I comfort myself by holding my face as close to Chase's as possible. I keep my eyes closed and inhale him. He is the opposite of smelling salts. The scent of him is so comforting and soothing it has ruined regular air for me forever.

Against all odds, we make it home. As soon as the car is safely parked in front of our apartment, I tell Craig that he's a war hero. We carry Chase inside and set his car seat in the middle of the quiet living room. We say to him, "Welcome home, sweetie." He does not respond. Craig and I sit down side by side on the couch and stare at him for a while. Craig finally says, "What are we supposed to do now?"

"I have no idea," I reply. "I think we're supposed to, like, give him a life."

"Okay," Craig says. "We can do that."

We take off our coats and get to work.

~

During our first week as a family, we sit on the floor in front of our sliding glass doors and watch the snow fall. When we touch the glass and feel the cold, we're surprised. We are so warm inside together that we have forgotten what cold feels like. We play soft music and listen to Chase's coos and gurgles and when the phone rings, we're startled because we have forgotten that anyone else exists. I warm Chase's bottles on the stove and notice the clock still announcing the time. The reminder that time is passing amuses me. There are no people other than we three, no world other than our apartment, no time other than Chase's time, and no path other than the well-worn one from Chase's crib to his bathtub to his rocker to our hand-me-down couch, where we huddle together in one corner and stare at each other long into the night.

When it's time for me to return to teaching, I leave Chase at day care and then cry at the sight of his empty car seat in the rear-view mirror. All day at school I am untethered. Without the weight of his soft body in my arms I feel like I might float away. One day his sitter meets me at the door and announces, "Chase rolled over for the first time today!" I look at her holding my baby proudly in the air and I feel like screaming. I am missing things. On the way home I call Craig and threaten to quit work, so he comes home early. We take Chase for a walk and stop the stroller in front of a bush with a bird in it. The bird chirps, right at Chase's eye level, and Chase laughs for the first time. Craig and I are stunned. We look at each other with wide, wet eyes. Chase's laughter sounds like a waterfall of crystal bubbles. His laugh is like music class when I dragged the felt-tipped xylophone mallet gently from the long, deep bar all the way to the tiny, tinkly one to hear every note in rippled succession. It's like a full rainbow of sound stretching from one corner of the sky to the other. Before this moment, Craig and I have not truly understood Chase to be a whole person, separate from us, capable of being delighted by the world around him. Craig and I hold each other and cry right there in the courtyard while Chase looks away from the bush, up toward us, and laughs and laughs.

We three are living so close to the surface of ourselves that it seems easy to touch each other. There is so much laughing and crying during that first year of our son's life. The laughter and tears are each of us bursting through our own skin to get to one another.

~

Craig, Chase, and I fit together perfectly. We strengthen each other like a braid. But as Chase grows, Craig and I are left alone with each other more often. Without Chase present, we begin to unravel. I am a child of Disney, so I learned early that a wedding is a woman's finish line. I thought all I needed to do was cross that wedding-day finish line and I'd finally be whole and content. I could sit down, brush my long pretty hair, plan my outfit for the ball, and never feel lonely again. Happily ever after. But I'm married now, and I'm still lonely. Loneliness after marriage isn't what I've been promised. I wonder if we're doing something wrong, if marriage isn't taking hold for Craig and me. I long for the depth, passion, and connection with Craig that I assumed would magically come with *I do*. And if this magical husband-and-wife bond isn't going to materialize, then I at least want to build a solid friendship. The problem is that none of my relationship-building strategies seem to work with Craig.

In all my close friendships, words are the bricks I use to build bridges. To know someone I need to hear her, and to feel known,

I need to be heard by her. The process of knowing and loving another person happens for me through conversation. I reveal something to help my friend understand me, she responds in a way that assures me she values my revelation, and then she adds something to help me understand her. This back-and-forth is repeated again and again as we go deeper into each other's hearts, minds, pasts, and dreams. Eventually, a friendship is built—a solid, sheltering structure that exists in the space between us—a space outside of ourselves that we can climb deep into. There is her, there is me, and then there is our friendship—this bridge we've built together.

This process seems foreign to Craig. Instead of taking my words in, thinking them over, and building upon them, he seems to let them bounce off of him and fall away. His responses are so disconnected from what I've just said that I have to fight the urge to touch my mouth and say, *Is this thing on? That is not what I meant at all.* It's as if I'm offering my thoughts into a void, so every effort I make to be known by him is wasted. I am handing him bricks and he's dropping them. One night I read this in a book about two lovers: "They could have a whole conversation with just one glance between them," and it makes my stomach lurch with longing. Craig and I can't even have a whole conversation when we have a whole conversation. Without that, I don't know how to reach him. I don't have any other building materials. Without a bridge to step out onto between us, I feel stuck alone inside myself.

We also seem to be missing a foundation upon which to build. In my other relationships, this foundation is shared memory. Craig and I don't have a shared memory because Craig seems to forget what I reveal to him about myself and my past. One night I sit on the couch, cruise the television channels, and settle on *The Newlywed Game*. The host asks the husbands, "What is your wife's favorite color?" "What was the name of your wife's childhood pet?" The TV husbands know these things about their wives and I know these things about Craig, but I'm certain Craig doesn't know these things about me. Craig wouldn't be able to smile and tell the host that his wife's favorite color is sky blue or that her first pet was a calico cat named Coco. He couldn't reach into his heart and pull out the story I told him once, about how Coco abandoned her kittens in my closet and how I nursed them all through the long nights with an eyedropper and how only one survived. He would not be able to explain that I named that kitten Miracle and that Miracle thought I was his mother. When I told Craig that story, I knew it was important, but he didn't. He smiled and nodded and then let it slip away. When I mentioned Miracle months later, Craig said, "Who is Miracle?" His forgetfulness feels like carelessness, and his carelessness feels like rejection. What do I do? Tell Miracle's story again? Do I say, *The story I'm about to tell is important to me. Please pay attention and remember it. Please keep this piece of me somewhere safe so we can build upon it?* Each day, we're making sandcastles I know will be washed away. I long for something solid, lasting, strong between us.

As an act of mercy, I decide to keep conversation with Craig at an operational level. I quit asking, "Are you sure you're really listening to what I'm saying?" Continuing to request something he can't offer feels unkind, like handing him a puzzle I know he can't solve. So I try to adjust my expectations. I stop bringing up world issues, friendships, the book I'm reading, my confusions about the past, and my dreams for the future. Instead, we talk about logistics—what time Chase ate or slept; what we'll eat for dinner; when my parents are planning to come visit; the weather; work. We are polite and gentle with each other, like two people having coffee for the first time. This feels like a significant and dangerous adjustment. It seems like we've stopped working to build a shared life and simply retreated back into the safety of ourselves. Instead of making peace, we are keeping the peace. We are avoiding conflict, but I'm getting lonelier and more afraid. Having something to say and no one to hear it is so lonely. Expecting less than true friendship in my most important relationship is so depressing. Every day when Craig gets home from work, I want to grab him and say, *I'm in here—I'm offering myself to you—do you hear me?* Instead, when he asks me how I am, I say, "I'm fine, just fine."

Conversation is my building material; Craig's is sex. To know someone, to love and feel loved by her, he needs to touch her and be touched by her. Craig uses his body exclusively and desperately, like I use words. He is like a blind man grasping to make sense of his world with his hands—he is constantly grabbing for me, rubbing me, pulling me close to him. When he reaches for me, I stiffen reflexively and then try to relax, to be receptive, to seem grateful for his attention like I'm supposed to be. I want to be a good wife. But my body's already revealed the truth. I don't feel grateful; I feel resentful. Every time Craig stops me for the affection he needs, I'm *doing* something. I'm taking care of Chase, the house, the meals. I resent the constant interruptions, and Craig's affection seems like a means to an end. It doesn't feel like he's pulling me toward him because he loves me, but because he needs sex to relieve his stress, and affection is the first step toward sex. I wonder how Craig would feel if people walked into his office every few hours requesting shoulder rubs to take the edge off. I want to say, *Leave me alone! I'm done doing favors today! I'm used up, overwhelmed by touch and needs already—why must you be needy, too? You're a grown man! Can't you help take care of business around here instead of creating more business for me to take care of? There is a child to be cared for, papers to be graded, laundry to be folded. Help me,* I want to yell. *Don't require more from me!* I say none of this, because I'm ashamed of my coldness and selfishness. I deflect his advances like he deflects my words, my stories. He is handing me bricks and I am dropping them. I know he's hurt by it. "What's wrong?" I ask.

"Nothing," he says. "I'm fine, just fine."

We know we need help, so we attend a marriage retreat where we're told that *date night* is the answer. I quickly realize that date nights require three things: conversational skills, sexual chemistry, and money. Since we have none of these, date nights highlight our problems instead of fix them. We sit across from each other at dinner and Craig scrambles for conversation topics while I anticipate the inevitability that he'll want sex later. I resent the transactional nature of this phenomenon—dinner for sex—and I annoy myself with all my resentment. *Why can't I feel desire instead of duty?* The answer doesn't matter. This is part of the deal. I have come to understand that sex is an inconvenient but important favor wives do for husbands to keep things running smoothly. I find the whole system strange but doable, like making sure the oil in the car is changed so we can get where we need to go. When we return from our date, Craig sends home the sitter and I prepare for duty.

I undress in the bathroom and then slide underneath the covers to wait. Craig joins me, and as things move along, I try to stay present and feel something. But instead of love, I feel apathy. I'm as lonely with Craig on top of me making love as I am with him beside me making conversation. Craig seems to be getting a job done and I am just lying there, waiting it out, making whatever noises seem to help speed up the process. I can't tolerate the acting, so I slip out. Now I'm hovering above my body, detached, separate, absent, watching sex happen to me. Craig continues on. He is not bothered by my apathy or absence, which makes me angry. Is he failing to notice that I've slipped out or is he failing to care? Now I don't just feel used up, I feel *used.* And so, from above, my mind begs my body to push him off, to curl up into a ball, and reclaim itself. My mind is silently screaming to Craig, *Get off get off get OFF.* But my body delivers a different message. My body is committed to keeping the peace. My body knows that we just have a few minutes left here, and we'll buy ourselves another week. So it sacrifices itself once again by pretending. By making movements and noises that communicate: *Yes, I'm enjoying this.* Sex feels like a betrayal of myself. Sex feels like a lie.

When it's over, we lie in bed together. I am lonely, afraid, and ashamed. I'm lonely because Craig has no idea what has just happened inside of me even though he was inside of me when it happened. I'm ashamed and afraid because I feel incapable of offering or accepting love. Every once in a while, we try to talk about it. I tell Craig that I'm struggling, that something feels off about our sex, that I know it's me but I don't know how to fix it. Craig is sympathetic but he has no answers. I can tell that he feels rejected. He wants to be inside my body like I want to be inside his mind. But he can't find me inside my body because that's not where I live, and I can't find him inside his mind, because that's not where he lives. He looks at me with sad eyes that say, *Look. I'm here. I'm offering myself to you; do you see me, do you feel me?*

~

One night, Craig passes by the couch and heads into our bedroom. "Come here," he says. My heart sinks and I stiffen. I can tell by his voice that he wants sex. I don't want sex; I want my bowl of ice cream and my corner of the couch. I'm so tired, but I stand up and follow Craig. I need to be a good wife so we can all be happy. Ten minutes. I promise the couch I'll be back in ten minutes.

But when I get to the bedroom, Craig is not grinning at me with the covers pulled up to his chin like he usually is. He's on a step stool, reaching into the closet. I sit down and wait while Craig pulls down a black plastic box filled with old VHS tapes. He carries it over and places it on the bed next to me. I know this special box because I carried it from the moving van into our apartment. These are the tapes that document the earliest part of Craig's lifelong soccer career. He keeps them because before Chase and me, soccer was the most precious thing to him. Craig seems nervous and I'm confused. Then he starts speaking quickly. He tells me that half of these are soccer footage from when he was a child, but the other half are porn. My eyes widen and I suddenly feel very awake. I look down at the box and I don't like the idea that all these childhood tapes are mixed with pornography. My first thought is, *These should be in separate boxes*. Craig asks if I want to watch something. "Soccer or porn?" I ask.

"Porn," he says.

"Together?"

"Yes."

"Do couples do that?"

"I think so."

I desperately want to say, *No, thank you*. I tell myself that I cannot always have what I want. Marriage is a compromise. "Okay," I say. I lie down on the bed and stare at our tiny TV while Craig gets the video ready. I'm wearing glasses and I suddenly feel self-conscious about them. People watching porn should not be wearing glasses unless they are sexy librarians. I look down at my flannel pants and hoodie and fuzzy heart socks and I cannot imagine that anyone could look less like a sexy librarian than I do. I wonder if it would be weird to ask if I can go get my ice cream first. I cannot imagine that rocky road and porn go well together, so I decide against it with great resentment. Why can't Craig just be happy with food like I am? Food is the reward; sex is just more work. I do my best to smile.

Craig lies down next to me and props himself up with a pillow. He decides that there is still too much light in the room so he gets back up and hits the switch. He comes back, and the video begins. Two women are making some kind of delivery to a man's apartment. These two women have bleached-blond, frizzy hair and they are climbing stairs while wearing stiletto heels. I feel immediate camaraderie with these women because climbing stairs in those things is harder than it looks. First there is some dialogue that feels exactly as forced and awkward as the dialogue Craig and I try to have before making out. Then the sex starts. My eyes widen and I try very, very hard to be serious about this. I do not try hard enough. I burst out laughing, but it's not because I think any of this is funny. It's just that my fuzzy socks are between me and the screen so I have to see both the socks and the sex at the same time. These two things together feel absurd. Craig looks over at me and he laughs, too, but it is a fake laugh. I can tell he's trying to figure out whether I'm laughing at the people on the screen or at him. I stop laughing. As soon as I stop laughing, I feel sick to my stomach. The man on the screen is telling the women in the stiletto heels exactly what to do and they are doing it, but they look very tired to me. And the faces they are making look angry. I wonder if Craig notices how tired and angry they look. Maybe not, because it is clear that the angry faces they are making are also supposed to be sexy faces. For a moment, I am relieved to see that anger and sex and exhaustion and duty are all mixed up here, too. I feel like I understand these porn stars.

At some point, the porn does to me whatever porn is supposed to do. I am transformed from a tired mom into someone who really, really wants sex. Now we are having sex. It is frantic. I notice that during this sex I am more engaged than usual. It is sort of animalistic. I notice that I am not thinking about Craig. I am thinking about the people in the video. This baffles me. Why am I thinking about the repulsive, sad, angry, frizzy sex instead of being present in this sex with my own gorgeous husband? I consider the strangeness of using one body to have an experience with another. The saying "neither here nor there" enters my mind. Then I wonder if Craig is thinking about the frizzy sex, too. Is this why his eyes are closed and he seems so distant? Is he neither here nor there? Is he with me or them? I think, *Why does he need them? Why does he need those angry, tired women? He's got one right here.*

Afterward Craig and I lie next to each other and stare at the ceiling. We are trying to figure out what to say next. Craig leans over and makes a face that is sort of a smile and leans in for a kiss. It feels awkward. Kissing seems too tender, too personal to follow what just happened between us and the TV. This kiss feels like an apology or a request to start over. After the kiss a mixture of fear, loneliness, shame, and darkness fills me. This familiar combination yanks me backward.

I am back in college. It's Friday night and there's a party raging. I'm in the basement with my boyfriend and eight of his frat brothers. My boyfriend has one arm around me and he is showing me a bag of cocaine. He's kissing my cheek and whispering in my ear. He is being gentle and attentive and his friends are all smiling at me, which is not how any of them usually behave. Now I'm leaning over the mirror on the coffee table and I'm doing my first line. My eyes are widening and my boyfriend is laughing and squeezing my leg. The rush starts at my head and goes all the way to my toes. The guys' faces light up and they cheer. They look at me with adoration. It is thrilling and half the thrill is from the coke and the other half is from the approval of these men around me. I can see that I'm one of them now. I'm a girl, but I'm cool. I'm so *cool.* Thank God. Before the coke I felt lost, but afterward I'm found. By these guys. By my boyfriend. By the coke.

For years, doing lines with them turns out to be the perfect fast track to their love. And when there is no coke, there's pot, so we get stoned and sit together with nowhere else to be. And if there's no pot, there's booze, so we drink and become witty and brave together. And if there's no coke, pot, or booze—there's food. If I'm ever left alone with no one to fold into, I can always eat. Bingeing keeps me numb until the night falls and I can ingest my love and belonging and courage again.

It's an effective but unsustainable system, because the higher I get each night, the lower I sink each day. In the early hours of the morning, the fraternity basement empties. People pair off to go home together and they take their drugs and love with them. Eventually, it's just me and my boyfriend in bed and he starts to fall asleep. This means aloneness is near. I cannot allow that to happen so I suggest sex, which buys me a few more minutes of love. But then he passes out and I'm left alone after all. So I lay my head on his chest, wrap my arms around myself, and settle in for my punishment: being wired, alone, in the damning quiet for hours—until the light slips in. Every morning, I watch the light from the merciless sun fill the room. My eyes dart from the blinking TV to beer cans to mirrors to razors to bongs to girlie posters to all the other remnants of debauchery. How did all of this seem glamorous a few hours ago? How did this ever look like love? The light breaks the spell, and it all looks like hell. My breathing shallows and panic sets in. *I don't belong here. How did I get here? How do I get out? How do I get back to my family? I don't want to be cool anymore. I want to be good. I want to be good.* Every single morning, I am a little girl who has woken up and discovered that she is alone and freezing in the dark woods. Every single morning, my terror is fresh and immediate and total. This is how I lived until Chase came. The dark of night was for blissful forgetting, the light of morning was for terrible remembering.

Now, for the first time since I became sober, I feel like that girl lost in the woods again. I'm lying in bed with my head on my husband's chest, but he's disappeared already. He's fallen asleep and taken his love with him. I'm alone now. The effects of the porn have left me wide awake and my eyes are darting from the blinking TV to the box of tapes on the floor. Suddenly our bedroom seems dark and dangerous. I am trying to figure out what just happened to us. What do we want that we think porn will get us? Coke had been a fast track to love. Pot, a fast track to belonging. Booze to courage. Food to comfort. Porn to what? Other people's bodies to what? What were we using porn for that we couldn't find in ourselves or each other?

The next morning I wait for Craig to wake up and I say, "I can't do that anymore."

He looks surprised and says, "Okay. I thought you enjoyed it. I

thought it turned you on." My stomach clenches at the phrase: turned you on.

I say, "No, yes. I guess it did, sort of, but not in a good way. It felt dangerous, dark. I can't get those women's faces out of my head. They just—their faces reminded me of my face too many times. Last night the porn was the coke and you were my ex-boyfriend and I was the girl I used to be. I can't be that girl anymore. I have a baby now. I want to be a mom and a wife. I just want to be good. I need real. I need to stay in the light. I just want it out. Can we get it out of our house? Can we not have this stuff in our house again? Just, please. Get it out of here."

Craig looks alarmed and tender. I can tell he has no idea what I'm talking about, but I can also tell that it doesn't matter. He says, "Yes, yes, of course. Don't worry. I'm sorry, baby."

And I say, "Promise me, no more."

"I promise. Consider them gone," he says. I am grateful. He wants me to be okay more than he wants what he wants. I know this. I love this man. But I still feel afraid. It's something about how the tapes were all mixed together in that black box and how it was animal sex and how Craig is now holding me so tight but won't look me in the eye. I sense danger. And I'm surprised and ashamed by this thought that arises: *I love you but I can't go back into the woods for you. I am on a path now and I have to keep walking forward. Chase needs someone to follow, and I can't carry you, too. So much depends on me.*

Later that morning when I walk into the kitchen holding Chase, Craig turns away from the eggs he's cooking and smiles at us. It's a sheepish, questioning smile. I walk Chase over to him and Craig puts down his spatula and wraps his arms around us. This hug is our acknowledgment of last night and our agreement not to discuss it again. We will put that box of darkness away and carry on with what we're good at: family.

~

We have two baby girls. We name the first one Patricia, after my mother, and the second one Amanda, after my sister. Tish and Amma. Sisters. We get ourselves a mortgage and a minivan. We find a church. Who could ask for more? Life at home with three kids is rich, bursting at the seams with love, but I am stunned by the amount of work that caring for my children requires. I quit teaching to stay home with them, and their needs are relentless. From dawn to dusk and then through the night I am reacting, responding, juggling, dripping with children. I am running a never-ending relay race, and since I am the only runner, I keep passing the baton back and forth to myself. My exhaustion is total.

Craig and I decide that our best chance of survival is to divide and conquer, so we laugh and cry together less often. Craig does his part by working all day and helping with the kids in the evening. Even so, I feel resentful. When he tells me about his long work lunch, I say, "I had the crusts from the kids' grilled cheese for lunch, and I ate it standing over the sink." When he mentions an article he read, I tell him how difficult it is for me to imagine having time to read an article. When he returns from his evening networking event, I ask if *networking* is the fancy word for drinking beer with other people who happen to have jobs. I'm embarrassed by my bitterness and worried because we are slipping further away from each other and deeper into ourselves. When we were three, we were one world, but now Craig has the outside world and I have the world of our home. We cannot bridge the two.

Every evening Craig walks through the door, smiles hopefully, and says, "How was your day?" This question is like a spotlight pointed directly at the chasm between his experience of a "day" and my experience of a "day." How was my *day*? The question lingers in the air while Amma shoves her hand in my mouth, while Chase screams, "Mommy come help me!" from the bathroom, while Tish cries in the corner because I never, ever, ever let her drink the dishwasher detergent. I look down at my spaghetti-stained pajama top, unwashed hair, and gorgeous baby on my hip, and I want to say:

> How was my day? It was a lifetime. It was the best of times and the worst of times. I was both lonely and never alone. I was simultaneously bored out of my skull and completely overwhelmed. I was saturated with touch—desperate to get the baby off of me and the second I put her down I yearned to smell her sweet skin again. This day required more than I'm physically and emotionally capable of, while requiring nothing from my brain. I had thoughts today, ideas, real things to say and no one to hear them.
>
> I felt manic all day, alternating between love and fury. At least once an hour I looked at their faces and thought I might

not survive the tenderness of my love for them. The next moment I was furious. I felt like a dormant volcano, steady on the outside but ready to explode and spew hot lava at any moment. And then I noticed that Amma's foot doesn't fit into her Onesie anymore, and I started to panic at the reminder that this will be over soon, that it's fleeting—that this hardest time of my life is supposed to be the best time of my life. That this brutal time is also the most beautiful time. Am I enjoying it enough? Am I missing the best time of my life? Am I too tired to be properly in love? That fear and shame felt like adding a heavy, itchy blanket on top of all the hard.

But I'm not complaining, so please don't try to fix it. I wouldn't have my day or my life any other way. I'm just saying—it's a hell of a hard thing to explain—an entire day with lots of babies. It's far too much and not even close to enough.

But I'm too tired to say any of this. I'm a windup doll that's run out. So I just say, "Our day was fine." Then I hand the baby to Craig, pull my dirty hair back into a ponytail, step into some flip-flops, and grab my purse. The kids notice that I'm preparing to leave and they start to cry and wrap their little arms around my leg. I kiss the tops of their heads, whisper, "Mommy will be right back," and extract myself from their grip.

I walk outside, climb into our van, shut myself inside, and breathe deeply. I drive to Target and wander the housewares aisles. I see a woman there with two toddlers in her cart and I want to walk over and say, *Excuse me. Is this the best and worst time of your life? Are you scared of your anger and your love? Do you have trouble talking to your husband? Do you feel heard, seen, known by anyone? Are you getting lost in there, too?* But I can't say any of that, because we have all agreed to stick closely to the script. There are only a few things we are allowed to say to each other, so I choose one of them. I smile and say, "Your babies are beautiful." She smiles back and I notice exhaustion and longing in her eyes, but I tell myself I'm projecting. I turn away and keep filling my cart with things I don't need that I'll return later. Bulimic shopping, my dad calls it. As my cart gets fuller and fuller, I tell myself, *You are a mother and a wife and you are sober and those are your only responsibilities on earth. You have everything you've ever wanted. Be grateful.* The truth is that I am grateful, but I'm also confused. We have done what we were supposed to do. We have become a family. But becoming a family has not made me unlonely.

~

Craig and I are good parents, but we are not good friends or lovers to each other. I wonder if this is because I chose the wrong man and Craig chose the wrong woman—or maybe because we didn't choose each other at all. I wonder if Craig believed I was the right thing instead of the right one. I wonder if we'll divorce after the kids leave for college, since we'll have nothing left to talk about. I wonder if we should just keep having kids, so we won't lose our glue. I wonder what it would be like to be married to a poet, to stay up late into the night discussing ideas and art, love and war, with enough passion and traction between us to fight loudly and make up tenderly. I wonder if my friends have with their husbands whatever it is we're missing. I wonder if everyone has what we are missing. Mostly, I try to stop these wonderings as soon as they begin. Wondering about true love and good sex feels like touching a hot stove. Considering these impossibilities burns and hurts, so I recoil quickly. There is no point in wondering *what if* or *what else* because I will never leave Craig. He's a good man, a devoted father, a gentle husband. I need to be grateful. I'll stay lonely for the rest of my life if it means my children have a family. I can't have it all. What we have is good enough. I stop reading love stories, and this helps me stop wondering.

7

ONE DAY I PASS by my computer with Amma in my arms and notice that some of my Facebook friends are participating in something called "25 Things." They're posting lists of interesting facts about themselves and I think, *Maybe I could make a list, too.* I consider that this might be a way to reach people outside my home, to complete a sentence, to tell the truth, to prove to myself and others that I still exist. *Yes*, I decide. *I do want to make my own list.* I put Amma down for a nap, sit at the computer, and start typing:

> #1. I'm a recovering bulimic and alcoholic, but I still find myself missing bingeing and booze in the same twisted way a woman can miss someone who repeatedly beats her and leaves her for dead.

I sit and stare at the words I've written: stark, bold, and unapologetic. I feel thrilled. *Yes. There I am. Right there.* That's not lost Glennon or found Mrs. Melton. That's not my representative. That's the real me. I want to learn more about me, so I keep writing. My fingers are flying now, pounding against the keyboard like they've been waiting a lifetime to be freed. They type juicy, dangerous, desperate sentences about marriage and motherhood and sex and life—it all pours out fast and furious, like the real me is gasping for air, like she's trying to get it all out at once in case she's never allowed to surface again. As I finish and stare at my writing, I feel more like I'm looking into a mirror than I have ever felt looking into an actual mirror. There I am, the inside me, on the outside. As I read and reread my list, trying to get to know me, I hear crying from upstairs. Amma is awake from her nap and she needs me. She'll have to wait because I'm finally awake, too, and I need me first. I'm desperate for other people to see this version of me, so I post the list to my Facebook wall and then climb the stairs to Amma's room.

An hour later I return to my computer. I look at the screen and scramble to make sense of what I'm seeing. My list has been shared publicly by friends and I have an in-box full of messages. I look at my wall and it's covered with notes from acquaintances and strangers. I feel sick, overly exposed, regretful. I've said too much and I want to take it all back. I shut the computer and walk away. Later that night I make a cup of hot tea, sit in front of the computer, and start opening messages.

The first is from a stranger. It reads, "I don't know you but I read your list this morning and I've been crying with relief for hours. Your list was my list of secrets. I thought I was the only one." I open a different message from an old friend: "Glennon. My sister is an alcoholic. None of us knows what to do for her." And another, and another, and another.

"My marriage is falling apart . . ."

"I don't know how to find my way out of this depression . . ."

"Sometimes I wonder if I'm not cut out for parenting. I get so angry that I want to push them down. I don't, but I want to. I feel like a monster."

I marvel at the honesty and pain. Many messages are from people I've known for years, but I'm discovering that I never really knew them. We've spent our time together talking about everything but what matters. We've never brought to each other the heavy things we were meant to help each other carry. We've only introduced each other to our representatives, while our real selves tried to live life alone. We thought that was safer. We thought that this way our real selves wouldn't get hurt. But as I read these messages, it becomes clear that we are all hurting anyway. And we think we are alone. At our cores, we are our tender selves peeking out at a world of shiny representatives, so shame has been layered on top of our pain. We're suffocating underneath all the layers.

~

The following week, my sister brings me a brand-new computer and says, "Write, Glennon. Get up every morning and write like the girl who wrote that list." I follow directions. Since a mother gets done whatever she'll lose sleep for, my alarm sounds at four thirty every morning. I stumble out of bed and toward the coffeemaker that Craig has preprogrammed for me. I take my coffee into the walk-in closet—my room of my own—and I open my computer and begin to write. Since it's dark outside and dark in the closet, I feel safe writing about my darkness. Just for this hour, I invite my real self forward to speak her pain, anger, love, and loss. I never miss this morning appointment with myself, because I can tell something important is happening in my closet. After I write, I feel calmer, healthier, and stronger. Every time I fling an internal demon onto the blank page, that demon turns out to be much less scary than I thought she was. I am becoming less afraid of myself. I wonder if this is because I need to check my shame levels daily, like a diabetic checks her insulin levels. Truth telling becomes my shame checker and my relief. It's a holy purging of the painful fullness of my secrets. And it's safe, because I'm purging in the dark, to a screen, so I never have to see anyone's confused or embarrassed reaction.

After a few months, I feel ready for others to see my writing, so I create a blog. Each morning, as I click the "publish" button and walk away to start the day with my babies, my mind is back at that screen. All day I wonder, *Will anyone read? Will anyone understand? Will anyone respond?* I am itchy for feedback. I check my blog a hundred times a day and find with delight that people are responding. They're responding from their homes and cubicles and phones and they're saying, *Me too, me too, me too. We see your dark and it matches ours. You are not alone.* Every new "like" and comment is a shot of adrenaline. I feel understood. I feel found. My blog community becomes my sanctuary, my safe world where there is no small talk, no script, only truth. Over time my blog goes viral and the agents start calling and I get a contract to write a book. Suddenly, none of my pain is wasted.

My desperation to know and be known by Craig relents. For the first time, all of my needs are being met—largely by strangers. I decide that this is healthy. It's not right to expect your every need to be met by one person, after all. I find myself writing about Craig instead of talking to him; it's safer and neater, and our story is tidier and better this way. We are easier to understand as characters than as real people. I can tell that Craig senses me slipping further away from him and into this new world I've created. He wants to come with me. He reads every word I write on the blog, and every comment others leave. He often learns the truth about his wife there first.

One day I write about falling off the wagon, because the night before I'd binged and purged after years of food sobriety. Craig reads it along with the rest of my community and writes to me from work. His e-mail says, "I just read your essay. I'm worried about you. Are you okay? Can we talk about these things?" That night, we sit awkwardly together on the couch and try to talk, but I don't know how to explain my bulimia or myself to him. There is no way to be as honest in spoken words as I can be in written words. I wonder why it's so much easier to be honest with strangers than with family. Sitting on that couch with Craig, I don't know how to be my real self. I feel like I'm still my representative. The real me is back in that essay and I just want to say, *If you really want to understand, can you just read it again?* Instead I say, "I'm okay, honey. I'm really okay, I promise." I stand up, signaling to Craig that the conversation is over. I do not need from Craig what I used to need. Through strangers on a screen, I've found the intimacy I yearned for. We both have, as I will soon learn.

I start to feel more tired than usual. Every morning my body feels pinned to the bed, like a butterfly in a glass box. My joints ache, my legs swell, and my hair starts falling out in clumps. I am constantly freezing. Two different doctors suggest that my illness is in my mind. I look at my swollen, bruised, skeletal legs and wonder, *Is my mind attacking my body? Is my body attacking my mind? Is something from the outside attacking all of me?* I don't know. A third doctor runs blood tests and finds evidence of chronic Lyme disease. I'm pumped full of so many antibiotics for so long that I'm in danger of becoming immune. I get sicker and sicker and we no longer know if I'm ill from the disease or from the treatment.

We buy a small sauna and put it next to our bed. My entire world becomes the two feet between my bed and the sauna. Some days I am so weak that Craig has to help me roll over. Aside from that, we rarely touch each other. My body is in perpetual pain and my mind is in a constant fog. I struggle to complete a spoken or written sentence. I often can't remember who or where I am.

One night I'm in bed, staring at the ceiling. I feel so heavy, like I'm sinking through the bed—down, down, and away. I lose consciousness. When I come to, I find the phone under the covers and try to lift it to my ear. It feels like a ten-pound weight. I dial my sister, and when she answers, I say, "I think I'm going to die soon. I'm so scared. What's going to happen to my family?" My sister is crying and I want to comfort her but I've already said all the words I can manage. I drop the phone. I hear my kids playing downstairs, and for the millionth time I lament the fact that I have lost the ability to care for them, to even be with them, maybe forever. I fade away and then come back. This happens to me several times a day and it is nothing like falling asleep and waking up—it is like dying and coming back to life. As I open my eyes, I see through a layer of fog that Craig is asleep beside me. I feel between this world and somewhere else. I want to tell Craig to take me to the hospital, but I can't move my hand to wake him up and I can't find the energy to form the words. I am trapped inside myself. In my mind I scream to him, *Take me to the hospital. Take me to doctors and experts and people who know how to help me!* He doesn't move, doesn't open his eyes, and I'm furious that he can't hear my silent scream. Now I'm fading away—no longer in my home but on my bed in the mental hospital, staring at the ceiling and telling Mary Margaret about canaries. I'm saying, *We're not crazy, Mary Margaret. But we're in danger. If they don't listen to the first signal, the canary dies.* And now she's fading and I'm back in bed with Craig. I look at him and then scan our bedroom with my eyes. I wonder, *What is my body telling me? What's the poison in here? How do I get us out of this mine?*

My friend Gena comes to visit and I am gray and small and wrapped in blankets. She is afraid for me. She and Craig plan a trip for our family to her condo in Naples, Florida. As soon as I step off the plane, the sun warms my face, the humidity hits my joints, and I feel relieved. After a few days, my knees stop aching and I stop finding clumps of my hair on my pillow. I find myself able to go on short walks and make my children sandwiches for lunch. On our last night in Naples, Craig touches my leg and I do not yelp in pain. He looks at me and says, "We should move here."

"Yes," I say. "We should." This feels right. We need to get away from everything except each other. We need time, space, sun, and palm trees.

Craig calls his boss the next day and says, "I'm moving to Naples to save my wife's life." His boss says, "Go."

I'm afraid because a health crisis is a hard time to move. I remind myself that since *crisis* means "to sift," a crisis is the perfect time to let the extra fall away so only the important will remain. We start to sift. We say good-bye to our kids' schools, our committees, our neighbors, and our church. We donate most of our things. Our responsibilities fall away like sand and by the time we arrive in Florida, we are left with just the children and each other. We promise ourselves that we will focus on rest, togetherness, and healing.

For months, we sit at the pool, shop at farmers' markets, and take long walks together. We resist new friendships and activities that might complicate our lives. Slowly, I get browner, stronger, and happier. The rest of the family follows suit. We are without structure for the first time. Craig is working from home and I am writing from home. There is no one to respond to but each other. Craig and I sit on our lanai together each evening, watch the baby alligator who lives in the lake float by, and say again and again, "I can't believe we did it. We are the people we used to be jealous of. We're free. This is our fresh start."

The flaw in this thinking is the fact that wherever you go, there you are. We did not escape the mine. We brought our poison with us. There is no becoming, only continuing.

8

One day my laptop gets a virus, so I log on to the family computer to write. I click on an unfamiliar file and an image of a snarling, naked woman crawling toward the camera pops up. I jump backward in my seat. I try to exit but every time I click the "x" another pornographic image lunges toward me, each more raunchy than the last. Now there are two women, naked and pale and kneeling side by side on a tile floor. A smirking man hovers over them with his hands on the back of the women's heads as he shoves both of their faces toward his penis. I try frantically to close the window, but now two women pop up, naked, kissing, clawing at one another while a group of men watch and laugh, like these two women are an inside joke among the men. These images feel designed specifically for men who hate women.

I gape at the computer as a paralyzing understanding washes over me: *I was wrong. I was wrong I was wrong I am wrong. I thought the rules were different in my family, in this little world I'd made. I thought I was safe here. But the rules are the same as they've always been.* I am back on the laundry room floor. I am back in line looking at a NO FAT CHICKS sign. I am sitting on the shoulders of a frat boy holding up my beer, singing, "We drink beer and fuck women and don't let other pussies get in." I am complicit in all of it. I am part of a system that agrees that women are for being implanted and teased and painted and then arranged and dominated and filmed and sold and laughed at. That sex is something that men do to women or watch women do to each other. Like these women, I am an inside joke to my husband. I click on a folder and there are more files, more women, a whole world of jokes being saved here. This is the computer our children use each day. I slam down the screen, shut my eyes, and shake my head hard. The discovery of what my husband has been bringing into our house makes me dizzy. Just like the black box mixed with Craig's soccer tapes and porn videos, my children's math games are mixed with these images. I grab onto the table's edge to steady myself as my mind explodes with fear.

What if the kids have already opened these? They'd understand that one of their parents saved these files intentionally. What would my girls have learned here about what it means to be a woman? What would my son have learned here about what it means to be a man? What would the faces in these images have taught my babies about how sex is supposed to feel? Oh God, they'd be poisoned. They'd have felt pain and shame, which is one too many layers for a child to carry. It occurs to me that saving pornography on this computer is like pouring whiskey into Amma's sippy cup. It is like leaving a few lines of coke in the playroom. Can't a parent be arrested for that? For a passing moment I actually consider calling the police. *Please take my husband away.*

I want to throw this pain portal into the wall and watch it shatter into a million pieces. Instead I push out my chair and run down the stairs and out the front door. I feel like sprinting away but my legs are weak, so I sit down in the driveway, cover my face with my hands, and scream. My behavior is as surprising to me as the images were, but this specific anger also feels familiar. It is as if this fury has been bubbling, slowly rising, and it's finally exploded to the surface. It feels primal, all-encompassing, and ancient, like a wildfire, sweeping and general and impersonal enough to burn the whole world. This indiscriminate rage scares me, so I decide to narrow it into a laser and point it directly at Craig.

As I sit there in the driveway with my head in my hands, I think, *We are in danger.* For the first time in a decade, my *we* does not include Craig. *We* is my children and me. *We* are in danger and Craig is the threat. And then I think, *What if this is all my fault? I was already cold and then I got sick. What if I've driven my husband to porn and I am getting what I deserve?* Then, just as quickly as the thought occurs to me, I reject it. *No. No, No, No. We are each responsible for our own sanity. He's weak. Fuck him. Fuck him. Fuck them all.* I decide I am done with Craig and done with men. But just as that decision brings a wave of relief, I think of Chase; how can I possibly write off all men when my son will grow to be one?

I steel myself and walk back into the house. I stay away from

Craig until after we put the kids to bed and then I enter the bedroom and say, "I found all of your porn. You promised to never bring that shit into the house again. You not only brought it back, but you put it right on our kids' computer. You're a dangerous liar. Do you even love us?"

Craig doesn't try to defend himself. He doesn't suggest that I'm overreacting. He hangs his head and says, "I'm so sorry. I'm going to get help."

Craig starts therapy. We hardly talk about it and we stop showing affection and there is no mention of sex anymore. I can't open myself up to what I cannot trust, so I shut down to Craig. My body and my heart are now mine to protect. Craig and I become business partners, and our business is raising children. We are polite, as colleagues should be.

And then, of course, there's more.

A few months later, I'm being swallowed up by a big black leather couch in Craig's therapist's chilly office. My knees don't reach the cushion's edge, so my legs stick out straight like I'm a doll someone has propped up. I decide that if I can't make my feet reach the floor, it's best to pretend that I don't want them to, anyway. I pull my legs up toward my chest and wrap my arms around them. I am my own shield.

Craig has told me that he discussed the porn with this therapist. His therapist sympathized because he'd almost lost his wife for similar reasons the previous year. Now this therapist is sitting four feet from me and I don't like the looks of him. I know how we try to save others in order to keep saving ourselves. I don't want to be part of this man's quest to save himself. Plus, he's jumpy and awkward and he keeps smiling hopefully at me—like he needs my reassurance that everything will be okay. I have no idea if everything will be okay, so I keep my face neutral. I am used to smiling at everyone on earth, and it is clear that this man is accustomed to being on the receiving end of women's reassuring smiles. I can tell that my refusal to put him at ease is throwing him off. He clears his throat and says, "Hello, Glennon, thank you for joining Craig here today." I feel jarred by the sound of our names pouring so familiarly out of this man's mouth.

The therapist goes on. "You look angry, Glennon. Would you mind sharing why you're angry?"

I want to say, *How do you know I'm angry? Because I'm not smiling? Craig's not smiling, either. Why does a woman's neutral face mean anger, while a man's neutral face means neutral?* Instead I say, "It's possible that I'm angry." He asks me why. I reply, "Because my husband has promised me for years that he's not watching porn, but he's been lying to me. Because he's been bringing porn into our home, where our kids might find it and maybe already have. Because he's putting my kids in danger. Because he's using the bodies of other parents' daughters to get off even though he has daughters of his own. And because for a decade he's been letting me believe that all of our sex problems are my fault. And maybe they're not. Maybe they're not at all."

The therapist looks at Craig. He's concerned about how Craig is receiving this. Craig is silent, sad, and distant. The therapist looks back at me and says, "I understand. But, Glennon, let's give Craig some credit. He's being honest. He's telling the whole story now."

The silence that follows the words *whole story* is electric and expectant, like the pause between lightning and thunder. The three of us look at each other and somehow, in that instant, I understand that the whole story is exactly what we're missing.

I flash back to two months ago. I'm standing at our kitchen counter and Craig is telling me about a friend of his from work. Craig says, "He cheated. It was really hard, but his wife eventually forgave him. They got back together. They're happy now." I'm surprised Craig is talking to me about this. I don't want him to. I don't want to talk about infidelity in my home, especially not while I am making lunches for my children. So I don't ask any questions. I don't look at Craig and I try not to listen too closely. But now, as I strain hard to remember Craig's voice, I hear the pleading tone there. I hear what I missed before: Craig is not just telling a story about his friend's marriage, he is asking a question about our marriage. I remember how I kept cutting my kids' sandwiches into perfect triangles, pressing down hard on the knife—slice, repeat, slice, repeat. I'd said to Craig, "Well, he's a creep and his wife's a fool. I'd take my kids and never look back. I'd never forgive that. Never, not in a million years."

Craig was quiet. "Yeah," he'd said, as he started clearing the table.

Now, in the therapist's office, I hear myself say, "Actually, I don't believe Craig is telling us the whole story. I don't think he's ever told the whole story."

The therapist's voice cracks when he replies. "Glennon, I hear you. But I know Craig and I believe he's being honest."

I shiver and pull my sweater tighter. For the first time I notice that both Craig and his therapist are wearing T-shirts and shorts. Why don't men ever notice the cold? Why don't they ever carry sweaters and curl up and make fists of their sleeves and wrap their arms around their legs? Why the hell are they so brazen and unfurled and warm and comfortable all the time?

"She's right," Craig says. "I need to tell her something." Craig's voice injects a deeper chill into my veins.

The therapist is scrambling now. "Okay, apparently there is more Craig needs to reveal. There is a right way and a wrong way to do this. Craig and I are going to meet a few times and then we will reconvene to discuss this new information in a few weeks."

I explode into sudden, loud laughter that sounds like gunfire peppering the quiet room. Both men jump and I am pleased. A woman's laughter grabs a man's attention faster than tears ever will. I point at the therapist and say, "Ha! That's funny. You said *right* and *wrong!* You are a funny guy!" I stop laughing as abruptly as I began. "No, there will be no reconvening. Craig is going to tell me everything *now.*" I look at Craig and feel ice for him. Sharp ice. Icicles. I say, "Start talking. If you leave out anything I will leave you and never look back. You know I'm capable of that." I stand up from the couch and walk across the office. I sit down in a chair as far from Craig as possible.

He looks away from me and starts talking. The first words he says are, "There have been other women. They've all been one-night stands. The first was a few months after our wedding."

I stop breathing. I'm staring at Craig and he's waiting for me to respond, but suddenly I'm not in this therapist's office. I'm holding my dad's arm, walking down the aisle. My dad and I are getting closer and closer to Craig. *Stop! Stop!* I am screaming this warning to myself and my dad: *Turn around! Go back!* But we are still walking. It's done. None of this can be changed.

Craig keeps talking, saying things that can't be true. While I've been home changing diapers, doing dishes, and feeding our children, he's been sleeping with other women. While I've been begging my body to heal, he's been lying down with other bodies. While I've been apologizing for my inability to connect during sex, he's been connecting with strangers. For years, he let me take all the blame. He let me cry on his shoulder and ask: *What is wrong with me? Why can't I feel safe during sex?* He patted my head and said he didn't know. He knew. He was the reason.

When Craig seems finished talking, we all sit still for a moment. The men are between me and the door. I will myself to stand up and walk toward it, but my legs refuse to carry me. The therapist looks concerned. He says, "Glennon, are you okay?" I consider this to be the stupidest question ever asked. I do not attempt to answer. I glare at him and silently dare him to say my name again. I red-hot hate him. I turn my chair away from the two men and toward the floor-to-ceiling window facing the parking lot. I lean over and put my hand on the window to steady myself. I look down into the parking lot and see a blond woman hurry to her van. I wonder what she knows about her people and what she doesn't know at all. *I hope you really know your people*, I think. But quickly I consider that maybe it's better for her not to know. During the past few minutes I've gone from not knowing to knowing, and so far knowing is much, much worse than not knowing. I am not certain that this knowing is even survivable. I take back my wish for her.

As she drives away, a scene from one of my favorite movies enters my mind. It's the sword fight between Inigo Montoya and Westley in *The Princess Bride*. There is a moment when Inigo recognizes that Westley is a skilled swordsman, just like he is. Inigo's face lights up in a fleeting expression of surprise, then fear, then wide-eyed respect, then finally settles into an amused expression that says, *Well, he might kill me, but at least this duel is going to be interesting.* I laugh again. Awkwardly and bitterly. For the first time, I recognize Craig as a formidable opponent. I thought I was the dark one. I thought Craig was simple, true, golden. But it turns out that he is a dark, skilled swordsman after all. He's just been hiding his tremendous capacity to inflict pain. *Ah*, I think, *here you are. Well played. I underestimated you. You're a complicated character after all, and things are about to get interesting. En garde.*

Behind me I hear Craig's therapist ask, "Why now, Craig? Why did you decide to share this today?"

I can barely hear Craig as he whispers, "I've been watching

Glennon. She writes and talks about her problems. She tells the truth about who she is. She says truth telling is how she got healthy. She leaves in all the bad stuff, and people still love her. I just want to know if maybe I can have that, too. I just need to know if she can really know me and still love me."

On tiptoes, I swivel my chair around to face the two men. I look at the clock on the therapist's wall above the window. Time is still passing. The kids will be waiting in the carpool line in fifteen minutes. For a moment I allow myself to wonder what their faces will look like when they find out that their family broke while they were painting rainbows at school. Then I shut that thought down. That pain is a pothole in the road that I need to sidestep so I can do what needs to be done. I push myself up and out of my chair. I pull off my sweater and hold it in my hand. I will my body not to shiver. I stand up, and the men's eyes lift toward me in unison. I look down at the therapist first and I say, "You should get an adjustable chair in this office so female-size people can put their fucking feet on the ground."

Then I look at Craig and say, "I have no idea if you can ever 'have that, too.' I just know you won't get it from me. To me, there is no 'you' anymore. Whoever the hell you are—you've destroyed our family and I will never forgive you. Never. I'm leaving now to pick up my kids. Come get your stuff tomorrow while they're at school, then stay the hell away from us. You're poison."

I pick up my purse and sweater and walk out the door, through the long hallway, and back outside. Then I become the woman hurrying to her car. I wonder if there is another woman in an office above watching me, wondering if I really know my people, trying to get her feet to reach the ground.

~

It's bright, warm, and orderly outside. I stand still to let my eyes and mind adjust. I feel like a tourist who's just stepped out of the airport and is finding her bearings in a new land. The blue of the Florida sky is blinding and every sound—an egret, a muffler, a passing plane—feels sharp and foreign. The sun's heat on my skin surprises me. Warmth still exists; that's interesting. I beg myself to stay present and pay attention. I need to notice more than I noticed before. The old me missed so much. Her happiness and peace were based on distraction and fantasy. This new me is traveling alone and can no longer afford to be distracted. Reality. Only reality. *Figure out what is real, Glennon.* My eyes feel propped wide open. My back is straight and my chin is raised, like a soldier. My lungs feel like they could hold gallons, like I've just inhaled smelling salts. Everything stings, but I'm awake.

I arrive at my minivan. It's still sturdy, boxy, gray, and dependable—just as I'd left it. But as I put my hand on the door, I taste hot hate in my mouth again. I pull back and realize quickly that I despise this minivan. I take a step back to gain some ground between us and I stare while the van morphs into a symbol of my decade-long loyalty, sacrifice, and naïveté. The van screams: *I am a wife! I am a mom! This is who I am! I might not be flashy, but I love my life!* Everything about this minivan is proof that I'm a fool.

I think about tossing the keys into the sewer behind me and

walking away from the van forever. But since I am a mother, dramatic gestures are off-limits. I must be steady. I must be calm. I must think about my children, who haven't yet seen the wave that's about to hit. I must be the steadfast captain of our sinking ship. I must smile as we go down so everyone can drown peacefully.

I climb up and into my horrible van. For the first time, I notice how little dignity is involved when a small woman must climb into a large car. *Why doesn't anything fit me, damnit?* I stare at the mess of coloring books, chapter books, applesauce containers, and dried Play-Doh on the van floor. I wonder if my kids will eventually look at this stuff like I'm looking at my van—like they're quaint relics from an old, distant world. I wonder if they'll see this mess with their new, wide-awake eyes and think, *Oh, right! Coloring books! I remember when my biggest problem was staying inside the lines! And, Mom, remember the minivan? Remember when your biggest problem was getting us to soccer on time? You used to worry about finding my cleats, remember?! That used to be on your to-do list: Find the kids' cleats! Coloring books and minivans. We were so precious, weren't we?*

I start to drive. I stop at a red light. I remember where to turn. A couple crosses the street and I smile and wave them on. I am surprised and proud of my smile. *Look at me. The worst has happened and here I am, calmly steering my car, smiling at strangers.* This smile is how I know I've become two people again. I am the one who has just lost her entire life and I am also her representative—driving, smiling, and waving. I have officially become a *We* again.

Pain splits us into two. When someone who is suffering says, "I'm fine, I'm fine," it is not because she is fine, it is because her inner self told her outer self to say the words "I am fine." Sometimes she will even slip and say, "We're fine." Others assume she's referring to herself and her people, but she is not. She is referring to both of her selves: her hurt self and her representative, the one fit for public consumption. Pain transforms one woman into two so that she has someone to walk with, someone to sit with her in the dark when everyone else leaves. I am not alone. I have my hurt self, but I also have this representative of me. She will continue on. Maybe I can permanently hide my hurt self and send our rep out into the world and she can smile and wave and carry on as if this never happened. We can breathe when we get home. In public, we will just pretend forever.

I stop at another red light and now my legs begin to shake, gently at first, and then harder until they're bouncing against the steering wheel. I will them to stop, pressing hard against them with my hands, but they only shake more violently. I wonder if the inside me heard my plan to hide her and now she is refusing to become invisible. I wonder if she controls my body after all. I have lost control of my life, my family, and now my own body. The light is going to change soon and I am panicked. My body is shouting at me to tell someone the truth. I steady myself the only way I know how: I call my sister. She answers on the first ring. "Hi, Sister! What's up?"

I say, "Can you sit down? I have to tell you something but don't worry—the kids are fine. I think."

"Wait, what? What's going on?" She sounds panicked.

I say, "It's not just the porn. Craig's been sleeping with other women. Since the beginning. One-night stands." My legs stop shaking. The light turns green. I put my foot on the gas and move forward, slowly.

My sister is silent. Then she says: "Oh my God. Oh my God, Glennon. Where are you? Are you driving? Are you okay?" She waits for an answer. This *Are you okay* question confuses me. It will be asked of me a thousand times during the coming year and it will mean something different each time. I use my sister's voice and context to translate *Are you okay?* to *Are you going to drive off the road right now? Are you going to hurt yourself or anybody else?* I answer, "Yes. I'm okay. I am calm. I'm going to get my babies and take them home."

I hear my sister say, "Get them home and stay there. I'll be on a plane to you tomorrow morning. I'll tell Mom and Dad tonight." Wait. She's going to tell my mom and dad? If we tell them, we can't take it back. If they know, this will officially be real. I try to imagine my parents' faces when they hear the News. They've already been through this with my sister. Her first husband wasn't who we thought he was, either. Craig is the one we trust. How will any of us trust anyone again? How will my dad accept that he can't protect either of his daughters? How will my parents be able to handle being duped yet again? I'm afraid that if I ask any of these questions, if I try to say too many words, my hurt self will sneak out through my throat, start screaming, and never stop. I swallow hard and say, "Okay. Fine. Do that. I'll call you later." I hang up.

I arrive at school and pull into the carpool line. I look into the vans of the other smiling mothers and I feel jealous of every single one of them. The teachers are outside waving and I wave back and then I see my babies, clutching their artwork from the day. When they see me, their bodies bounce up and down and their faces crack open into huge smiles. Their smiles are real. They are not split into two. I look at them and my heart plunges so low, so deep that I can't imagine it will ever be recovered. *Those faces. One thing. I promised to do this one thing right. To give them a family. Stability. To protect them from pain. I have failed. They will be hurt in ways I've never been hurt. Nothing is as they believe it was. How can I avoid all of this being true for them?* They bounce into the car and I want to hold them tight, but I smile, make my eyes bright, and I say, "I love you! How was your day?"

The littlest leans forward to kiss my cheek and she says, "It was great! How was yours?"

"It was great, honey. Just great."

I tell the kids that Daddy had to leave for a last-minute trip. When we arrive home I make a cozy nest for us on the couch and turn on the TV. They are thrilled. TV on a school night! I look at them and marvel that just yesterday, I would have worried about TV on a school night. *We were so precious, weren't we?* Now I just feel grateful that we've survived the all-out attack the world waged on us today. I feel proud. I have rescued my babies and brought them home and now they are on my couch, safe and sound, and it is only the four of us that matter. The storm can rage on outside, and we will be safe here forever in our bunker. I bring them their chicken nuggets, sit down next to them, and pull Amma onto my lap. I breathe in her hair. I make a silent promise to her and her brother and sister that all will be well. *We are fine. We really are. We don't need Daddy, after all.*

This initial numbness and denial is shock and it is a gift. Shock is a grace period. It gives a woman time to gather what she needs around her, before the exhaustion and panic set in like a heavy snow. Shock allows her time to circle her people so that she can enter the hard work of grief, which will require all of her. Shock is the window offered after the fall so a woman can prepare herself for winter.

Two hours later, I take the kids to the bathroom and help them brush their teeth. *Look at us, brushing our teeth under these circumstances.* I am amazed at us. I take them to their rooms and tuck them in one at a time. As I kiss the girls good night, the velvet of their cheeks levels me. They are so young, so new. Their skin is this soft because nothing has toughened it yet. The sun hasn't blistered it, wind hasn't hardened it, toxins in the air haven't gotten inside, and adolescent hormones haven't seeped out. Nothing has happened to them yet. Their skin is perfect, unspoiled, like their hearts. I have protected their skin and hearts so they have suffered nothing alone. That is over. Soon I will have to tell them things that will send their hearts on journeys I can't travel with them. Their hearts will crack and harden and toughen before their skin does. This is not the correct order of things.

I look at them and understand that when they learn that Mommy and Daddy might not stay married, I will lose them a little bit. We were one, but soon shock, grief, and loss will split us. In fact, we are already split—they just don't know it yet. And I will not even be able to hold them while they cry and say, *I know how you feel.* I do not know how it feels to be a child whose family shattered overnight. I do not know. My children are nine, six, and four years old. How can I let them suffer something I've not suffered myself? I am supposed to walk in front, clearing the path for them. But I can't lead anymore because I don't know where we're going. I begin to feel like I can't breathe, so I back away and stand in the hall, trying to gather my strength. I hear my girls giggling and whispering. They weren't asleep after all. I feel shocked by their joy, like I've just detected signs of life underneath hopeless rubble. After they hear their news, will my babies ever giggle again? Will I?

I walk into my bedroom. I stop in front of the bed and stare. My eyes rest on the dent in Craig's pillow and then on his book, still open on the bedside table. I quickly flip his pillow and shove his book underneath the mattress. I need to unsee his things so I can forget he exists. My breathing is getting shallow again. Shock—my saving grace—is wearing off. Now the room is spinning and I'm becoming frantic. The questions begin grabbing at me like icy fingers: *What if we divorce? What if Craig remarries? What if my babies call another woman mother? What if she doesn't love them? What if she does? What if they don't love her? What if they do? How do I unknow what I know? How do I make all of this not true?*

My legs have stopped working and I'm on the floor now. I crawl to the wall and pull myself up against it for support. I lean forward and put my head between my knees to quell my nausea. I try to steady my breathing. Concentrate on breathing, Glennon. Just breathe. I look at the door and remember that it's unlocked and I crawl over toward it, reach up, and lock it. The kids can't see me like this. I'm all they have. After the door is locked, I prop myself up against the wall again and rest my head against it. I close my eyes for a moment. This feels familiar, this position on the floor. My mind travels back to Mother's Day, 2001.

There I am, on the bathroom floor, cold tiles against my thighs, holding a positive pregnancy test. My hands shake so hard I can barely make out the little blue cross, but there it is. I close my eyes tight, trying to unknow what is true: I am pregnant. I open my eyes and see the white, cold toilet I've spent half my life kneeling in front of. I've returned to it again and again to empty myself, to hide my messy humanness and flush it all away. The bathroom has been my hiding place and the toilet, my altar. This place has been my answer to the question of me for over a decade. But as I look down at that pregnancy test, I realize I'll need a new answer now, something less deadly to kneel before and hide inside. I'd found those answers in wifehood. In motherhood. These were better altars. Less dangerous. They made everyone I loved so proud and they were closer to the truth of me.

But maybe not true enough. Because it's ten years later, my back is against a different wall, and I'm staring at another life-changing truth that has come to take away the new altars I've painstakingly built. If the answers to the question of me are not successful wife and mother, then what answers do I have left? None. If I am not Mrs. Melton after all, then who am I? Nobody. The end.

I remind myself that ten years ago I thought my bathroom floor moment was the end. That little blue cross was my eviction, but it was also my invitation. It was an invitation to create a better life, to discover better answers, to build healthier altars, to find a truer identity. What if this eviction is some sort of invitation, too? But to where? Out of my marriage? To a life alone? Away from my children? No, no, no. I don't want this invitation. Not this one. The last one was toward Chase, toward Craig, toward Love. This one is an invitation away from what saved me. I don't want it. I don't want this beginning. I love my answers. I love my life. I am panicking now.

I try to remember how I found my breath ten years ago. What did I do first? How did I survive this? I went to a meeting. But I can't go to a meeting now. My kids are asleep and we're alone here. I drag myself off the floor and to the computer. Writing will have to be my meeting now. I will have to save myself this time. I start typing a list:

Questions I Can't Answer

1. *Will we ever be a family again?*
2. *Will I be a single parent?*
3. *Will my children be ruined by this?*
4. *Will my kids one day have another mother?*

I stop and look at that last question and my soul screams *No. No.* And then I add:

5. *What am I going to do?*

Then I start a second list:

Questions I Can Answer

1. *Am I loved? Yes.*
2. *Are my children loved? Yes.*
3. *Did I survive Rock Bottom before? Yes.*

I stare at the last question and remember something I just read—that the word *disaster* comes from *astro*: stars, and *dis*: without. This will only be a disaster if I lose all awareness of light. There in front of the computer, I feel darkness setting in. I need to find some light.

Quickly, I make one more list:

What I Know

1. *What you don't know, you're not supposed to know yet.*
2. *More will be revealed.*
3. *Crisis comes from the word meaning to sift. Let it all fall away and you'll be left with what matters.*
4. *What matters most cannot be taken away.*
5. *Just do the next right thing one thing at a time: That'll take you all the way home.*

I print out my three lists and climb into bed with them. I lie in bed and stare wide-eyed at the ceiling. One of the questions I can't answer keeps running through my mind: *What am I going to do?* I force myself to translate that unanswerable into an answerable. I change What am I going to do? to What am I going to do *next?*

I make a plan:

I will go to sleep. The sun will rise. I will make breakfast. I will take the kids to school. I will come home and rest.

As I repeat my plan again and again, my breathing slows and evens.

I will go to sleep. The sun will rise. I will make breakfast. I will take the kids to school. I will come home and rest.

Just the next right thing, one thing at a time.

I am so tired. I lean over and turn off the lamp, but I continue to clutch my lists like they're flashlights. I am bringing the light with me into the dark. I fall asleep holding my words. Words are the light I'll use to light my path. This is no disaster. This is simply a crisis. I will let myself be a child at the beach who digs in the sand and lifts her sieve out in front of her, watching the sand fall away and hoping that treasure will be left. I fall asleep.

9

I do not remember picking my sister up at the airport the next day. I do not remember my parents' arrival two days later. I do not remember telling the kids that their mom and dad love them very much, but need time apart. I do not remember telling Craig to rent his own apartment, or agreeing to let him take one of our dogs. I do not remember setting up a schedule for him to see the kids. Grief is an eraser. I feel erased of everything but pain and fear.

My anger is the ocean. There are moments of calm and stillness and then, without warning, the disturbance begins beneath my skin, churning, gathering power until there is nothing I can do but surrender and ride it out. I stand in my driveway and scream into the phone at Craig, wishing him dead. "Dead would be easier than this!" I shout. "Dead would mean I wouldn't have to deal with you again. I could tell the kids you were a good man and grieve you and start over with someone else. If you were dead, I wouldn't have to share these kids with you. The kids that I protected and you threw away. It's selfish for you to even exist anymore!" When the wave of fury subsides I am wiped out, exhausted, spent.

My imagination is a jack-in-the-box. I'm constantly ambushed by images of Craig with other women and these visions leave me breathless. I picture myself calling Craig on a business trip, his cell phone ringing unanswered on his hotel night stand while a naked woman lies beside him. I imagine my children talking to their friends at school, "So our stepmom's taking us to Disneyland. . . ." Often when these ghosts pop up, I'm literally knocked off balance, so I have to grab for the nearest wall to steady myself. I cannot even trust my own mind to be kind to me.

My depression is a dark, dense fog. When it clears I emerge to engage with the kids, but then it rolls in again without warning and I find myself unable to speak or move. I pass everything off to my parents and get into bed and sleep. This is my parents' gift to me, the gift of sleep. Sleep is my only escape, and the price of escape is waking up with the fresh awareness that I wasn't dreaming. This is my life.

My grief is a solid brick wall in front of me. I want to bulldoze through it, scale it, tear it down a brick at a time. I'm desperate to get to the other side of the wall so I can see what's waiting for me down the path. But the wall will not budge, or let me climb, or let me remove a single brick. All it will allow me to do is lean against it, exhausted. Grief is nothing but a painful waiting, a horrible patience. Grief cannot be torn down or scaled or overcome or outsmarted. It can only be outlasted. Survival is surrender to the brick wall.

There is no such thing as progress, or if there is, it's not linear. Every day, I wake up and march the same lap of grief, rage, and panic. While I'm marching, tender memories sneak up on me. Craig and the kids on my birthday morning—giggling and tiptoeing into my bedroom in T-shirts Craig had made with pictures from our wedding day; Craig's tears when he holds Tish for the first time; Craig waking me at midnight to show me that all three children and both dogs crept into our bed yet again. We did all of that together. We made a family. We've lost so much, and I miss all of it. But do I miss what we made or do I miss the man who helped me make it? I don't know. Like a pinball, I bounce back and forth between *go to hell* and *please come home.*

~

One day I sit on the beach with my parents, watching the kids play in the surf. I say, "I'm divorcing him."

My dad nods and says, "Some people stay their whole lives for their children and then when their partner dies they come alive. And everyone else, including the children, thinks, Why the hell didn't she do that before? She could have had a whole life. You do what you need to do. We have money saved and time available and we will be here." I look at my father and feel peace for a moment. I try to hold tight to that peace, but then my eyes wander to my children chasing each other down the beach. My peace falls away. *No, no. That plan won't work. That simply won't work at all. I can't lose them. I'll pretend forever if it means I don't have to break their hearts.*

So the next day I call my sister and announce, "I've decided I'm staying. I'm going to fight for this. I'm going to make this work."

She says, "Okay. I am here and will walk beside you every step of the way." I feel hopeful. *Yes! This is the answer!* But then I catch my reflection in the mirror and I think, *No. It won't work. Never. I can't pretend.* My hope disappears. I say to my sister, "Never mind. That's not right either."

She pauses and then says: "Maybe, for now, the only right decision is to stop making decisions."

She's right. She sees that I'm trying to fix my pain with certainty, as if I'm one right choice away from relief. I'm stuck in anxiety quicksand: The harder I try to climb my way out, the lower I sink. The only way to survive is to make no sudden movements, to get comfortable with discomfort, and to find peace without answers. I don't know. The truth is that I just don't know what will become of us.

There is only one strategy I can count on during this time, and it's the same one that helped me get sober: *Just Do the Next Right Thing, One Thing at a Time.* I can never glimpse the end of the path, but if I squint hard, I can see the next step. The way I squint is to sit in the quiet for a few minutes every day, block out all the other well-meaning voices, and say, *Give me today my daily bread. I don't know what will happen tomorrow, but today, give me enough energy and wisdom and strength and peace to handle what comes. Help me ignore the big decisions, which will make themselves, and just help me focus on the small ones.* And then, just for the day, I try to do what feels true, trusting that the next day I'll be given a fresh batch of whatever tomorrow requires of me.

~

Day after day, the still, small voice insists that the next right thing is to stay away from Craig. I do not want this to be true. I want the voice to let us off the hook. But when I am quiet, my deepest wisdom insists that leaving Craig means staying with God and truth and light. Going back to Craig—using the security of our relationship to avoid my fear and loneliness—would be abandoning myself. Self-betrayal is allowing fear to overrule the still, small voice of truth. This is the only thing I cannot do. I can do the second hardest thing—leave Craig, face the crumbling of my family, try life alone—so that I don't have to do the impossible thing: betray myself. If I want to know: *Is there anyone on earth who won't betray me?* I must answer myself: *Yes. Look in the mirror. She won't betray you.*

So my question in the quiet shifts from *Will I ever be able to trust Craig again?* to *Will I be able to trust myself?* This is the critical question. So I do the hard thing. I build trust with myself. I want to be the kind of person who will take care of me.

God and I know what to do, but my knowing wavers when I try to explain myself to others. When a friend asks, "What happened?" I want to pick up a crystal vase and smash it into the ground. *That's what happened,* I'd say. The few times I try to tell the shattering as a story, I regret it. Spoken words make what happened to us too tidy, too palatable, too ordinary. I can't describe the ferocity of the fear and rage inside me with words tame enough for the light of day. When I finish the telling, I want people to be as shocked and confused as I am. I want thunder to roll and mouths to drop open. But most often, the listener makes the pain harder for me by trying to make it easier for her.

If the receiver of my story is a Shover, she listens with nervousness and then hurriedly explains that "everything happens for a reason," or "it's darkest before the dawn," or "God has a plan for you." Standing inside the wreckage of my marriage is too uncomfortable, so she uses these tired platitudes like a broom to sweep my shattered life into a tidy pile she can sidestep. She needs me to move forward, to make progress, to skip through the hard parts and get to the happy ending. She needs to edit my story so that it fits inside her story about how good things happen to good people and life is fair and things tend to work out nicely in the end. *I see what this is. This is an opportunity for greatness! The biggest challenges happen to the strongest people, after all! This will be a blessing, you'll see.* With these declarations, she puts her hands on my back and shoves me toward the door of hope. I don't want to be shoved. I want to turn toward that door in my own time. But she can't stand waiting, so she steps into the spotlight and becomes the hero of my story. I wither in the face of her optimism and clarity and slink offstage. *Yeah. I guess you're right. Everything happens for a reason.*

If she is a Comparer, she nods while "listening," as if my pain confirms something she already knows. When I finish she clucks her tongue, shakes her head, and responds with her own story.

Comparers need to deflect my personal pain by refusing to accept that any of this is personal. So instead of making a new file for my story, she files me into some category for which she already has a reference. She tells me how we are the same, she and I, because she had a bad breakup in college. Or how actually, I am more like her friend Jody, who went through something "just like this." So I find myself listening to a story about some lady named Jody—nodding, coo-ing, oh no-ing, poor Jody-ing. My hopelessness is too intense, so the Comparer's strategy is to hijack the moment. *Let's make this about Jody—because dealing with you right now is too much to handle.* And so I become just another story in a long line of stories and my family becomes just another family. My children become *just like Jody's poor children* and my husband is *just like Jody's husband.* But the paradox of pain is that it is only universal in retrospect. In the present, it is fiercely personal. In the immediacy of my fresh grief, I am nothing like Jody, and Jody's pain is nothing like mine. But this is the Comparer's show now and she insists it is all the same. Only special people have the right to grieve, and my story just isn't all that special. She refuses to be surprised. This is nothing new. Just ask Jody.

The Fixer is certain that my situation is a question and she knows the answer. All I need is her resources and wisdom and I'll be able to fix everything. She tells me that I just need to pray harder. I need to be more sexually available. I should leave. I have to stay. I really, really need to read this amazing book that worked miracles for her friend. The Fixer insists that there are definitive ways in and out of this mess, because to consider it random means that her life is also vulnerable to disaster. *No, no, no.* There is a foolproof marriage formula and her security is dependent on believing that Craig and I simply haven't followed the formula. I don't have the energy to tell her that I've attended the same conferences and read the same books she has. I do not have the heart to suggest that maybe life doesn't respect the boundaries of our tidy formulas, and that knowledge is not a fortress that keeps out pain. "Sure," I say. "I'll be sure to read that book. Thanks."

The Reporter seems far too curious about the details of the shattering. There is a line between concerned and excited, and the Reporter steps over it. She asks inappropriate, probing questions and her eyes glisten as she waits for the answers. She is not receiving my story, she is collecting it. I learn later that she passes on the breaking news almost immediately, usually with a worry or prayer disclaimer. "You guys, I'm so worried about Craig and Glennon. Did you hear what happened? Keep them in your prayers." Our story is the only thing we have that is completely our own. A person who steals it and uses it to entertain is the worst kind of thief.

Then there are the Victims. A few people write to say they've heard my news secondhand and they are hurt I haven't told them personally. They thought we were closer than that. As if grieving people, upon hearing their news, begin making lists in descending order of how close they are to everyone they know so they can disseminate information in an orderly, fair fashion. As if etiquette exists inside grief. As if mothers dealing with shattered families are mostly concerned with how their friends feel about their pain.

Upon receiving messages from these Victims, I learn what the phrase "my blood turned cold" means.

And finally, there are the God Reps. They believe they know what God wants for me and they "feel led" by God to "share." Lord, have mercy.

A few months after we arrived in Naples, I filled out the kids' back-to-school paperwork and realized I had no one to list as their emergency contact. All of that freedom we'd wanted so badly started to feel lonely. Who'd bring us a casserole if we got sick? Before we moved we'd been a part of a church that felt like our village, a place where adults' faces lit up when they saw our kids, where we knew and loved their kids back. We missed it. We decided it was time to join a church, and we started attending one that advertised itself as young and hip. The first time we went, we were taken in by the coffee bar, rock band, and hundreds of young families who seemed like one big family. It felt like we could be folded in there. But gradually I began to feel less and less comfortable with the particular brand of comfort this church offered. For one, there weren't any women in leadership, or people of color in attendance. There also seemed to be an underlying political agenda that was heavy on defending the majority's rights and light on looking out for the poor and marginalized. The minister seemed more focused on the thriving of this institution than he was on the survival of those hurting beyond the institution's walls. I knew this church wasn't the right fit and planned to find a new one, but then Craig's news hit and I needed the comforting warmth of the fold.

A few weeks after the separation, a woman I know only vaguely grabs my arm in the church hallway. I smile at her and she cocks her head to the side, wearing a sympathetic frown. *Damnit*, I think. *Here we go.*

"Can we talk?" she says.

No, I think. "Sure!" I say.

She begins, "Our Bible study heard what happened, honey, and we feel led to talk to you about the dangers of divorce. Divorce is simply not God's plan for your family. We love your children like our own and we don't want them to suffer. God's preference is the nuclear family, and if you step outside of His umbrella of safety, He doesn't promise to protect you, honey. God gave you to Craig as his helper. Your duty is to help him through this time. There are a few scriptures God laid on our hearts to share with you, if that's okay."

She rustles through her purse and I stare at her steadily while my insides explode with flashing lights, red flags, and fury. My fury is for every woman who's been told by the church that God values her marriage more than her soul, her safety, her freedom. My fury is for every woman who has been taught that God is man and man is God. My fury is for every woman who has been told that her bad marriage is the cross upon which she should hang herself.

I hear myself say, "Excuse me. What is it that you think *happened?*"

"Well, you left, right?" While she waits for me to answer, her frown turns into a patronizing smile. I've never understood patronizing until this woman stands in front of me and insists that she doesn't need to know what happened to me to know the best way forward. She doesn't even want to know. It strikes me that more information is the last thing this institution wants women to have.

I look around at the walls of the church and it is as if, for a moment, the poison in this mine becomes visible to me. This woman is not speaking to me woman to woman; she is speaking to me as a representative of this institution. It is very important to this institution that she and I never know that there is a difference between leaving a man and leaving God. It needs us never to understand that there is a difference between submitting to God and submitting to patriarchy. So the secret that is kept under tight wraps in these places is this: God is the God of woman every bit as fiercely as God is the God of man. *There it is. The keeping of that secret is poison. That's why women stop singing here.*

I look away, farther down the hall, and I see Tish in line with her Sunday school class. Tish sees me and her face lights up. In that instant, I realize I owe nothing to the institution of Christianity—not my health, not my dignity, not my silence, not my martyrdom. I do not answer to this place, I answer to God, to myself, and to the little girl in that line. None of us wants me to try to pass off cowardice for strength, willful ignorance for loyalty, codependence for love. That little girl doesn't want me to die for her; she never asked to bear that burden. She wants me to live for her. She needs me to show her not how a woman pretends her life is perfect, but how a woman deals honestly and bravely with an imperfect life. She needs to learn from me that these four walls don't contain God and that the people inside them don't own

God, that God loves her more than any institution God made for her. She will learn this only if I show her that I believe it myself. She will know this only if I know it first. She will learn her song only if her mother keeps singing.

The still, small voice inside me arises and says, *Get the hell out of here*. I turn back toward the woman, and my eyes fall upon a picture above her of Mary and baby Jesus. I find my words. "Why are you so certain that God prefers the nuclear family? Judging by that picture above you, God chose an unwed teen girl to be God's mom. Maybe God has broader ideas of what constitutes a good family than this church does."

Her eyes widen and she says nothing.

I continue, "I left Craig because I know the difference between right and wrong, not because I don't. God and I talk every night, every morning, and sometimes every twenty minutes. Don't you think God is more likely to speak directly to me about me than to you about me? Good luck to you and good-bye. My girl and I are leaving." I gesture to Tish, and she runs out of line and into my arms. Her teacher asks her to return to the line and I smile and say, "No. I want her out of that line. She's fine. She's coming with me." We both turn our backs and walk outside into the fresh air and sun. We hold hands and laugh. We walk to our van together and we bring God with us.

I never go back to that church, and I stop talking to anyone outside of my family about my marriage. I stop asking for advice and pretending I don't know what to do. I do know what to do, just never more than one moment at a time. I stop explaining myself, because I learn that making decisions is never about doing the right thing or the wrong thing. It's about doing the precise thing. The precise thing is always incredibly personal and often makes no sense to anyone else. God speaks to folks directly and one at a time, so I just listen and follow directions. And when I need to work anything out, I turn to the blank page. There, no one can steal my pain or try to poison my knowing, and there I always have the final word in my own story.

10

SLOWLY THE MONTHS PASS, and even though I will it not to, Christmas comes. It's the first Christmas our family will spend in two homes instead of one. Craig and I are desperate to fake holiday cheer for the kids, so one night Craig delivers a tree. It is the ugliest Christmas tree I've ever seen—half-dead, droopy, and brown—a Florida tree. As he carries it inside, its brittle needles hit our tile floor like a steady rain. Craig makes hopeful, optimistic noises while arranging the frail branches and I allow my silence to speak for itself. I feel desperate to leave the room because the awkwardness is so painful. Even the Christmas music playing in the background sounds forced and hollow.

I ask the kids to begin unpacking the ornaments and I motion to Craig to follow me into the bathroom. We shut the door and he looks at me hopefully.

"I'm filing for divorce," I say. "You need to know that I don't intend to reunite. I am not in love with you. I don't trust you. There is not much I know for sure right now, but I do know this: I can never, ever have sex with you again. Our marriage is over. This is over."

Craig sits down on the edge of the bathtub, staring at me with wide eyes. His shoulders fall. He looks so tired. He rests his elbows on his knees and buries his face in his hands. He says nothing.

"I just got a Christmas card from a divorced friend," I say, holding out the card for him to see. "Look. Look at this. She's remarried to that guy. The husband is remarried to that woman. All their kids are there. They are all together on Christmas morning. We will be like that. We will never be the same, but we will find a way to be loving. We will forge a new, bigger family and we'll give the kids a good life."

Craig is silent for another long moment and then he clears his throat and says, "I am not remarrying, Glennon. I am not moving on. I am never giving up. I don't want that Christmas-card family. I want my family." He is crying now. "I found a new therapist and I'm going twice a week, Glennon. I'm working so hard. I'm trying to make it better. I am going to become the man you and the kids deserve."

"You should be in therapy and you should become the best man you can be—you owe that to yourself and to our children. They deserve to have an honest man for a father. But don't do this work for me. If you do this for me you're wasting all of our time. I'm done. I'm gone, Craig. I am never, ever coming back. You need to move on."

He is bawling now. "Okay, Glennon. You go ahead and move

on. Take care of yourself. I understand that you need to. But you can't force me to. No matter what you do, I am not giving up. I am going to keep showing up every day and taking care of you and the kids because that's all I know how to do. That's who I am. You and the kids are all I have and all I want. If it takes me the rest of my life, I'm going to keep trying to win you back. And if I don't, it won't be because I stopped trying. I will never stop trying."

His tears do not soften me, they disgust me. His tears are too late. They are for himself, not for us. "Then you will be wasting your life, Craig."

"It won't be a waste. Even if it doesn't work, it won't be a waste. Fighting for you and the kids will never be a waste."

"These words. They're just words. You know that, right? They mean nothing. They mean nothing to me."

"I know," Craig whispers. "I know."

We walk out of the bathroom together, smile for the kids, and decorate the tree.

~

One afternoon I open an e-mail from my friend Lynn. It says: "I got your message. I support your decision completely. How is life so far without him?"

Since this will be in writing, I feel able to answer her.

> It's hard. Right now it's not the emotions that are taking me down, it's the logistics. I thought that Craig and I had a good division of labor in our marriage, but I think what we really had

was a division of power. I don't know how my life works, so I feel powerless all day. I don't know how to fix our air-conditioning and we're melting in here. I don't know where our money is or how much of it there is or if our bills are getting paid. I don't know how close I am to the limit on my credit card because I don't know the limit on my credit card. Apparently our entire life runs on passwords: our bank, the kids' medical records, everything. I don't know the damn passwords to my own life. The car stalled today and someone stopped behind us. It felt dangerous to let him help, but what choice did I have? The kids and I have become completely dependent on the kindness of strangers.

Also, we can't eat anything from a jar because I can't open jars. When I try, I end up in furious tears because, *Damnit—I should be able to do this.* I know the kids are thinking, *This is why we need Daddy.* And last night I finally got the kids to bed and I was tired all the way through to my bones, so I melted into the couch. I picked up the remote and I couldn't get the damn thing to turn on the TV. Fifty buttons on that thing and not one button said "on." I felt so desperate. Without booze, TV is all I have to take the edge off. At night, I need a mental break from trying to solve this impossible puzzle that is my life. But I couldn't have my break, because I've never learned how to use the damn remote. I considered waking up Chase to ask him to help, but I couldn't suggest that he needed to be *the man of the house.* So I pushed every button six times and worked myself into a rage and considered smashing the remote into pieces. But I didn't. I just lay there on the couch and stared at the ceiling and wondered how many women return to crappy marriages simply because they really just want to watch some damn television at the end of the day. A lot, I bet. Who do you think makes those remotes? *Men.* The remotes are a conspiracy. The remotes are tools of our oppression. Some woman needs to invent a Liberation Remote. I'd do it, but I'm too freaking tired. The thing I keep thinking is, I have to learn these things so that if I ever remarry, it'll be because I want a partner, not because I need a handyman. So I'm trying to learn my life. I found the numbers of a mechanic and an air-conditioning company and I put them on the fridge next to a list of my online passwords. I feel a little stronger every time I look at it.

A week later I receive a package from Lynn. It's a rubber jar opener, and a note that says, "So we can always open our own jars."

~

Craig keeps the promise he made in the bathroom. He shows up. I walk out to the van in the morning and find it cleaned from top to bottom. I climb in and notice that the gas tank is full. I come home to piles of groceries on my front step. I open an e-mail from Craig listing the kids' upcoming dentist and doctor appointments along with a note saying he'll take them to everything so I can rest. He sends me lyrics from the Mumford & Sons song "I Will Wait" and says that every night he drives, listens to their album, and cries. I stop by the school and he's in the classroom, stuffing the teacher's envelopes or reading with the kids. One day I open the front door and find three wrapped birthday gifts for parties the kids are invited to that weekend. Underneath the packages is a note: *I can't stop being their dad or your husband, Glennon, even if I have to do it from far away.* His efforts feel different to me than they have ever felt before. He is loving us by serving us, and this kind of love feels steady, creative, and selfless instead of needy. I have told him there is no hope that I'll love him back, and he is loving me anyway. This isn't transactional love, because I am not reciprocating. This is interesting to me.

One afternoon I open the mailbox and pull out a letter addressed to Craig in flowery, female handwriting. I stand in the street and stare at the pink envelope for a moment. No return address. *Jesus.* Adrenaline soars through my body and I can't tell if I am terrified or excited. Is catching Craig in the act victory or defeat for me? I don't know if we are teammates or opponents anymore. I sit down on the grass and remind myself that if I open this, I will never be able to unsee whatever is inside. I swallow hard and tear open the envelope. Written on the page inside are three short sentences: *Craig, thank you for your commitment to our women and children. Your dedication and kindness are appreciated by all. The kids love you! With Respect and Gratitude, Donna.* The printed emblem on the card reads THE SHELTER FOR ABUSED WOMEN AND CHILDREN. I reread the letter several times. Then I go inside, call Craig, and read the letter aloud to him. "What is this?" I ask.

"I'm trying to be better, Glennon," he replies. "I'm just trying to learn. And when I can't be with you guys, I need to do some good."

~

The kids are seeing a therapist to help them with the separation. Even though I told Craig I was filing for divorce, something has kept me from calling a lawyer. Divorce is what I want, but it's not what I want. There is no decision that brings me peace. One afternoon in March, I go to the kids' therapist's office to discuss their progress. She says, "Glennon, you need to make a final decision about your marriage as soon as possible." She explains that kids can handle divorce or reconciliation as long as there isn't ambiguity.

I look at her and say, "So you're saying I should rush my decision?"

"Yes. I guess I am saying that," she replies.

It's bad advice. Hurrying certainty is never a good idea. But she seems convinced, and I feel relieved to be backed into a corner. I'm so tired. And I'm worried about my kids. Every day they ask me when Daddy is coming home and I haven't been capable of telling them never. I change my mind. I decide to invite Craig home.

Sometimes it's not love that brings a woman back—it's exhaustion. It's loneliness. It's that she's fresh out of energy and bravado and she's tired of being afraid of night noises she never even noticed before she was alone. Sometimes it's not the noises—it's the silence after the baby says a new word and there's no one to be amazed with. Sometimes a woman just needs her life's witness back. So she looks down the barrel of her life, sighs, and thinks,

Maybe a compromise is okay. Maybe too hard to leave is a good enough reason to stay. That's what I decide. *Love is not a victory march; it's a cold and it's a broken hallelujah.*

I call Craig that evening and tell him that he can move back in. I say, "We'll take it slow and try."

He is silent on the other end and then he says, "Thank you, Glennon."

He walks through the front door that evening, bags in hand, and the kids climb on him in the foyer while he holds back tears. He unpacks quietly, sheepishly, and as I watch him reclaim space in my closet and our life, I feel rigid, closed, and afraid.

That night I stay in the closet to change into my pajamas, keeping as many closed doors between us as possible. When I'm half-dressed, I hear Craig walking toward the door. My pants are down around my ankles and I am afraid he'll walk in on me naked. My heart thumps against my chest and I try to quickly yank my pants up over my knees, but I fall to the floor and hit my head hard. My cheek scratches against the rough carpet, my heart races, and I can't move because my legs are trapped inside my pants. I lie on the floor and as tears of frustration surface, I pray he won't come in and see me like this. When I gather the energy to stand back up, I pull my sweatpants up and my hoodie over my head so no inch of my skin is exposed. Even though it is only eight o'clock, I climb into bed. I curl up tightly, as close to the edge as possible. I don't want Craig to join me. I don't want to share my bed and my closet and my life with him. Instead of being a relief, Craig's return feels like an invasion.

The next morning, Craig takes the girls out to breakfast. Chase and I go to the local zoo and find ourselves standing in front of the lion's cage. The massive, majestic cat paces back and forth, muscles rippling under his coat, passing just inches in front of us. The lion stops and stares right at us. Chase and I stare back, entranced, silent, until Chase says, "He's so beautiful."

I whisper back, "Yes, yes he is. Isn't it weird that we can just stand here, noticing his beauty, without being afraid?"

Chase says, "Yeah. It's the metal bars." I hold on to one of the bars and think of myself crumbled on the closet floor and then curled up at my bed's edge. I consider how my fear and anger have skyrocketed, how the bit of tenderness I'd gathered for Craig has disappeared. I am terrified and angry again and that is because I've lost my bars. Living separately was keeping me safe. But now my bed is his bed again and my bars are gone and it is difficult to see any beauty in a lion or a man when you are terrified of being torn to shreds.

For two weeks, I try to build my own bars with extra layers of clothing, a turned back, cold shoulders, and scowls. I feel the need to protect myself by being distant and nasty, so that Craig will be constantly aware of my pain. But I can't show my anger often because of the kids. They need normalcy and hope. So one night I pull Craig aside and say, "If you see me smiling, don't take it as forgiveness. Don't take it as weakness. For God's sake, don't take it as happiness. Don't for a second hope that my smiles mean I'm *over it*. Every smile from me is an act for the kids. What I look like on the surface in no way reflects what's going on inside of me. Inside,

I'm angrier than I've ever been in my life. But I'll act because acting is the only choice I have left. You've even taken away my right to be honest with my face, my voice, my being. At least when you were gone I was honest. Now I'm just an actor. It was bad enough that you betrayed me, but now it's like you've forced me to betray myself."

And betray myself, I do. For two weeks I smile. I pretend. I send my representative into my marriage. I pat Craig on the shoulder while the kids are watching. I pour his coffee in the morning and laugh at his jokes at dinner. Inside, I feel like I did in my wedding night bed. Alone. Fearing I'll never feel safe with a man a day in my life. Wondering if I'll just be an actor forever.

~

One Sunday morning in June, I walk into the kitchen and find Craig making breakfast. The kids sing while Craig flips pancakes. Sunlight pours in through the window and music fills the room. It all looks idyllic and perfect. It looks too good to be true. I stand still and watch until Chase says, "Mama! Come over!" They all turn toward me with hopeful smiles and I understand that all I have to do in that moment is step inside, take back my role as happy wife and mother, hug Craig and with one look say, *Let's start over. Let's just forget. Let's be Mr. and Mrs. Melton again. I'll resume my roles of wife and mother so the rest of you can have your happiness back.* I want to be able to do that for them. I want to be able to make this okay for them more than I've ever wanted anything in my life. My mind understands stepping in to be the most practical choice and my heart longs to be held and loved and enveloped back into the fold of this family.

But the still, small voice won't allow it. The still, small voice insists that if I walk back in now, I'll be rejecting the gift inside of this crisis. Crisis. Sift. This is an invitation to allow everything to fall away in order to be left holding what can never be taken. The invitation in this pain is the possibility of discovering who I really am. Eleven years earlier, when I found myself stunned sober by that pregnancy test, I'd looked around and decided that adulthood meant taking on roles. Adults became and so I became, became, became. I became a wife and then a mother and a church lady and a career woman. As I took on these roles, I kept waiting for that day when I could stop acting like a grown-up because I'd finally be one. But that day never came. My roles hung on the outside of me like costumes.

Those roles I once used to clothe and define myself have been torn away. And that's why I wake up each morning paralyzed, disoriented, stripped, naked, exposed. Wondering, *Who am I?* Who was I before I started becoming other things? What is true about me that can't be taken away, that has nothing to do with the people I love or the work that I do? Who is the woman who will or will not step back inside of this family? That is the question that needs to be answered before I make this decision. I've only begun the work that needs to be done here. *Not yet,* the voice says. *Not yet. See this through. Unbecome, Glennon. Unbecome until you uncover who you really are.* And so I smile at my people and then I turn away and walk back into my bedroom. I lock the door.

I go to my computer and look up nearby beach hotels. I find one a few miles away, call the front desk, and discover that the rooms are much too expensive to consider. I book a waterfront room anyway. I pull down my suitcase from a high shelf on the closet and pack a bathing suit, cover-up, pajamas, flip-flops, tea bags, three candles, and matches. I go back out to the kitchen and ask Craig if I can speak to him. He comes to the bedroom with me and I tell him, "I'm going away for a couple of days. I need to figure something out. And I need to be alone to do it."

"Okay," he says. "Go ahead. Take your time. I've got everything here covered."

Later that afternoon, I check into the hotel. I sit down in my room and look around. I resist the urge to turn on the television. I need to sit with the quiet; I know that much. I open the sliding glass doors that lead to the small balcony, lie down in bed, and fall asleep. Before I open my eyes the next morning, my ears awake to the sound of the waves hitting the sand. It stirs something inside of me. The sound of the water speaks not to my spinning mind or yearning heart, but to my still, strong soul. The water is speaking in a language I knew before the world taught me its language. I lie there and I let the sound of the surf massage my soul for two hours. I let it speak to me and I do not speak back. I just receive. I understand with great gratitude that I could rest here forever, offer the sea nothing in return, and it would never stop speaking to me. The surf is gentle and selfless and steady. This is not a transaction; it is a gift.

I feel the need to be closer to the water. I stand up, pull on a sweatshirt and yoga pants, and throw my hair into a ponytail. I gather a blanket from the closet and walk down the stairs toward the beach. I spread the blanket out on the sand right in front of the Gulf's rolling waves. Now, I can not only hear the water, but see it and feel the cool breeze on my face. Everything is aqua—wide open in all directions. As far as I can see, there is only sea, sand, and sky. I curl up and fall asleep on the sand. When I wake it is late afternoon and I feel hungry. I leave my blanket and when I go back to my room to make tea and gather snacks, I keep the doors open. I cannot stand to be separated, not for a moment, from the sea. I carry my tea and snacks back to my blanket and as soon as I sit down, the sun hits the horizon and its white light shatters into all the colors of the rainbow. Now I am surrounded by reds and blues and oranges and pinks, and the sky seems to curve around me like I'm in the center of a snow globe. The sky, the breeze, the colors, the warmth, the birds dancing in the surf, the pelicans trusting the sea for their dinner—all of this forms a message to my weary heart. I feel overwhelmed with love, with beauty, with attention and reassurance. I feel held. I feel safe.

The surf continues to hit the sand rhythmically and dependably and I trust it will continue. The sun is setting but I know it will rise again tomorrow. There is a pattern to things. This makes me wonder if I can also trust that there is a pattern, a rhythm, a beauty, a natural rise and fall to my life as well. I wonder if the one holding together this sky might also be capable of holding together my heart. I wonder if the one making this sky so achingly beautiful might also be working to make my life beautiful, too.

The top of the sun disappears into the water, and even as I watch it go, I know that I am the one doing the leaving. It is staying in the same place, shining on and on. I will just have to be patient and rest until I can see it again. Light disappears sometimes, but it always comes back. And after I say good-bye to the sun, I applaud loudly for the one responsible for the show. I'm flooded with awe, relief, and comfort. I feel a chill because the sun is down now. Everything is as it should be. All is well.

The other people on the beach start to leave, but I am not ready. I stay still, so I learn that the sky keeps exploding once the sun is gone. Deeper reds and brilliant purples continue to wrap around me like blankets until it all fades into pitch navy. Then I turn around and catch a glimpse of the moon, a silver boomerang in the sky that seems to have appeared out of the literal blue. But I know the moon's always there, too, waiting for its time to be seen. The day has to fall to make way for the night and the night has to surrender its place so the day can have its turn. This strikes me as a holy rhythm. I wonder if whatever created this rhythm of the tides and the sky and the sun and the moon has a holy rhythm for my life, too. I consider that perhaps I'm in the middle of a cycle. Maybe there is a time for everything. Maybe there is a timekeeper.

My eyes fall below the moon to the plants that line the beach, every shade of purple, green, and pink. I think, maybe some loves are perennials—they survive the winter and bloom again. Maybe others are annuals—beautiful and lush and full for a season and then back to the earth to die and create rich soil for new life to grow. Maybe there is no way for love to fail, because the eventual result of all love is New Life. Death and resurrection—maybe that's just the way of life and love. I decide that regardless of whether my marriage reveals itself to be an annual or perennial love, there will be new lushness and beauty and life that comes of it.

I can only see my toes through the white flashlight of the moon. I note that even at night, there is some light to see by. We are never without light. There is no true disaster. I find myself thanking the moon and the one who created it. I use the moonlight to gather my wrappers and my mug and my blanket. I stand up, look around, and notice I am the only one left on the beach. I've been sitting on the sand for eight hours. I walk back to my room and I do not stop to wash my feet at the fountain. I keep all the sand and salt attached to me. I need to bring it with me inside. I sit down on the bed, the sandy blanket still wrapped around me, and I call my mom. When she answers, I say, "Mama, I think I found something today that my soul loves. I sat on the beach for eight hours today. I listened to the surf and I felt like it was speaking to me. It was reassuring me or something, trying to show me how things work. And then when the sun set, I felt so held by the sky, like it was covering me and protecting me."

My mom says, "Oh, honey, that takes me back. You've loved the sound of the ocean since you were three. When we'd get close to the beach, you'd kick your feet against your car seat and squeal and we'd laugh and laugh. Then the second we got you to the sand, you'd take off toward the sea. Sand and water have always been home to you."

As she speaks, the tears come and they feel cleansing, like an organic baptism. There it is, something I've loved since I was three and will still love when I am eighty-three. Here I am, on a bed in a hotel room all by myself, meeting my self. I've learned one true thing about me. Maybe there is more to learn. *Hello, soul. I am learning what you love. I will get more of this for us. I promise.* I have met my self and I am going to care for her fiercely. At least as fiercely as I care for everyone else in my life. I will not abandon, ignore, or lose myself again.

I snuggle under the covers with more hot tea and start flipping through the channels, fast because of my low threshold for anything emotional. I settle on a home-improvement channel and start following the story of a couple who buys a fixer-upper sight unseen. After they move in, the nightmare begins. There have been leaks, water damage, and electrical fires. The couple is patching up problems one after another and they look haggard and afraid and their savings are close to gone. They seem to be running out of patience with their home, their life, and each other. They finally sit down with a contractor who says, "Your problem is that everything in this house is wired wrong. These walls look fine but there's a nightmare underneath. I recommend that you tear down the walls and rewire the entire house, or sell it and move on. Either fix the problems once and for all or leave it to be someone else's problem." The wife's face falls. She looks around at the walls she's painted so carefully and hung her family pictures on so lovingly. She is having a hard time accepting that inside her perfectly decorated walls hide problems dangerous enough to destroy her whole house. I understand.

She says, "I'm done with this place. Let's get out of here and start over. Let's buy a new house."

Her husband pauses and says, "But how will we know that the next house won't have the same problems? At least we know what we've got with this one. Once we tear it all up, we'll be able to see what's behind the walls. We can begin again, with experts this time. We can make it right. Make it our own. Let's stay." I watch the wife's face and she looks so tired. I fall asleep before learning what the couple decides to do.

The next morning I wake up to the sound of the surf again and I smile. I smile there in bed, alone. I notice right away that this feels like a new kind of smile. I'm not smiling because I am acting or because I have to, but because my soul recognizes something it loves. I am not paralyzed this morning. I know what to do with myself because I know one true thing about me. I climb out of bed, brush my teeth, and make my coffee. I walk back down to my spot on the beach and set up my blanket again. It's early morning, six o'clock, and everything here looks different and the same. Little birds run back and forth in zigzags, flirting with the surf. Pelicans swoop down, snatching breakfast out of the water. The air off the Gulf is cool on my skin while light slowly fills my beach snow globe. I am alone on the beach, and it feels decadent to be the only one witnessing all this beauty. It feels almost wasteful. I remind myself that it's not wasted, it's just all for me. I'm so grateful that I'm here to accept this gift.

I sit down in the sand and think about the couple on the television last night. I ask myself, *What if Craig and I are like that house? What if our wiring is bad?* I know I can't stay in my marriage, stare at the nicely decorated walls, and pretend all is well underneath. But if I leave, will I take my bad wiring with me? What if I need to tear down my walls and rewire? Is that what Craig's doing in therapy? Rewiring himself? I don't know. I don't know if Craig will be able to rewire himself, but it strikes me that if I don't fix my wiring, it won't matter what house I move into. I'll burn them all down. Sitting there, on the beach, watching the tide roll in and out, I understand that I've been hanging pictures on my walls hoping that'd be good enough.

"We can begin again," the husband had said. "We can tear down the walls and make it right." He wanted to move backward so they could move forward. I thought about how adamantly I'd been refusing to look backward. How certain I was that progress meant to move forward. To continue becoming. But what if I had to go backward first? What if progress meant unbecoming?

I don't know how to fix my marriage. All I know is that I need to tear down my own walls and face what's underneath. I cannot save my marriage but I can save myself. I can do that for me and for my children and for every relationship I have now and for every one that comes in the future. I can do that so when I make the most important decision of my life, whether to stay with Craig or to leave him, I'll know that it's my strongest, healthiest self doing the deciding. I look out at the sea, up at the sky, and down at the sand. I think, *I can be brave enough to tear myself down—because the One holding all of this together will hold me, too.*

When I get back to my hotel room I sit down at a little desk, pull out a piece of paper, and write another list:

1. *Start therapy—examine my wiring before I move.*
2. *Come to sunset three times a week.*
3. *Wait one year to make any more decisions.*

PART THREE

11

I STOP IN THE BATHROOM to check the mirror before entering the therapist's waiting room. My costume for this appointment consists of a blazer, suit pants, and heels. I look at myself and wish I'd chosen something else. I've lost weight and my pants hang off of me like I'm a two-dimensional cardboard cutout. My blazer swallows me and hides my hands, while the cuffs of my pants drag on the floor, covering my shoes. I do not look professional; I look like a child trying to look professional. I lean in to examine my face more closely. My cheeks are hollow, my eyes are dull, and the gray of my skin shows through my makeup. And my hair. Oh, God, my hair. I reach up to touch it, to prove to myself once again that my Rapunzel hair is really gone. It is. Still gone.

Weeks ago, I became obsessed with cutting off my hair. The night before my appointment, I e-mailed my friend Rachel to tell her my plan. She wrote back and joked, "I see! You're trying to save your marriage by becoming less attractive? Excellent plan!"

I'd written back:

For God's sake. I am not trying to become *less attractive*. I am trying to look more like *myself*. Why do we all have the same hair, Rachel? Who decided that to be attractive we needed this Barbie hair? Who decided we need to be attractive? I don't even know what I'm spending all my time and money trying to *attract*. I've been altering myself for so long to match whatever "look" is deemed hottest at the moment that I don't even know what I actually look like anymore. I am trying to figure out who I am under here. And by the way, I am not trying to *save my marriage*. My marriage was bullshit. I will either have a new marriage or no marriage—those are the only options. And this haircut isn't about anybody else anyway; it's about me. I'm like Thoreau. I'm trying to strip myself down to my barest essentials so I can figure out where I begin and where the woman the world told me to be begins. I'm going back to the starting line. I want to unlearn all the stuff that made me sick and angry. I don't want to come to the end of my life and discover that I never even knew myself.

Twenty minutes later Rachel replied: "Okaaaaay, well, I sure as hell hope you don't tell your poor hairdresser all that. That's a lot of freaking pressure. Cut my hair like Thoreau! Jeez. You okay, Glennon?"

"I don't know," I answered. I don't know.

The next morning, I walked into the hair salon, sat down in

my stylist's chair, and said, "Cut it all off, I want it short. Close to my head, please."

Kathleen's response was visceral. She put down her scissors and nearly yelled, "No! What? Why? Your hair is so pretty! We worked so hard to get it like this! Other women would kill for your hair! Is this about Craig?"

"No. I don't know. I think this is about me. I just . . . I just need to see myself." Kathleen softened.

"Okay," she said. "We'll do it. Should we look at a magazine to get some ideas for the cut?"

"No," I said a little too loudly. "No. I don't want to look like someone else. Just, whatever you think. I trust you. Just take it off."

"Okay," she said. She started cutting, and for twenty minutes we watched the waist-length hair I'd cherished like it was the only currency I had to spend drop to the floor. As I saw it fall away, no longer a part of me, I felt terrified and free. I didn't want to be Rapunzel anymore. I didn't want anybody climbing my hair to get to me any longer. When Kathleen finished, I stared at myself and felt fascinated and horrified. My first thought: *I am no longer pretty.* And then: *Maybe that's okay. I have other things to try to be.* Kathleen stared at me quietly. Her face was kind and concerned. She put her hands on my shoulders and I sat up straighter. I felt like she was trying to tell me she understood, and that she had my back. Tears pooled in my eyes and then in hers.

She said, "What do you think, G? Should we bleach it? Maybe platinum?"

"No," I replied. "It's fine. It's good. It's exactly what it is. I'm just going to look how I look."

"You look beautiful . . . strong."

"Thank you," I whispered. I paid my bill and drove home. When I walked in the door, my girls crumbled to our foyer floor. They cried and touched my head and said, "What did you do, Mommy?" *I broke the rules,* I thought.

But now, as I stare at my short hair, skeletal body, and oversized clothes, I realize that Kathleen was grasping. I don't look strong at all. I've simply traded one extreme costume for another. I've gone from Rapunzel to freaking Peter Pan. I pull out a tube of lipstick from my purse and paint some on. Now I look like Peter Pan wearing lipstick. I feel rage bubbling inside. *Why is it so hard to look like myself?* I stare at this red-lipped, short-haired, sickly looking woman made of cardboard and begin to feel light-headed. I clear my throat just to hear the sound, to prove to myself that this woman in the mirror is actually me. Hearing my own voice is comforting, so I clear my throat again. I'm in here somewhere. I look strange, but my insides are still me.

~

I check in at the front desk, sit down in a corner chair, and start planning my approach. I've been in and out of therapists' offices since my parents first discovered my bulimia. My goal has always been the same: Reveal just enough to be left alone. I considered therapy to be a victory if I could stay sick, if I could carry on with my eating disorder in peace. Today I feel different. I want to be healthy. I just don't know how. I feel like my heart is failing and I've been trying to perform heart surgery on myself. I need to lie down and have someone else work on my life for a while. I'm not here to insist I'm fine, I'm here to say *uncle*. If I had a little white flag I'd raise it. Here I am. Help. Please know what to do. Please let this woman I'm about to meet know what I should do.

I'm brought back to my senses when the door opens and a woman wearing a crisp, modern, white pantsuit appears in the waiting room. While she scans the room for me, I examine her. Her eyes are as smart as her suit. She looks more professional than warm—like a woman who is ready to get down to business. She is not wearing any makeup, and this leads me to conclude that we are kindred spirits, which is odd, since I am wearing four pounds of makeup. I think of myself as a woman who does not need or care for makeup but just hasn't gotten started with that yet. I analyze her and decide two things: I like this woman and I'm afraid of her. I lower my invisible white flag. I am no longer worried she won't know what I should do, but that she *will* know what I should do. What if I tell her everything and she decides I have to leave Craig? What if she decides I have to stay? I feel both desperate for and unprepared for clear answers.

The woman's eyes rest on me and she says, "Glennon?"

"Yes," I say. "That's me."

"Welcome." She smiles. "I'm Ann. Follow me." Ann leads me through a hallway and into a small room filled with books. She closes the door behind us, points me toward a chair, and hands me a bottle of water. Then she sits down a few feet from me and picks up a notebook and a pen. She says, "So, what brought you here? Tell me your story."

Oh, God, what the hell is my story? What's the opening scene? Did it start on my wedding day? Did it start when I was ten? I watch her pen hover over the page. She'll start forming her opinion of me with whatever I say first. *Control the story, Glennon, control the story.* Then it occurs to me I'm too tired to be the author of my life anymore. I just want to be the reporter. And so I begin by reporting what I'm thinking exactly now, here, in this moment, right where I am.

"My husband has been sleeping with other women. I hate him. I want to stop hating him but I can't. I don't feel safe in my own home. I'm angry all the time. Not just at him but at everything, especially men. Why do they throw away their families for sex? I hate sex. No matter what happens, I'm never having sex again. I'm afraid all the time, too. I'm afraid of staying together. I'm afraid of divorcing. I can't even think about my kids' pain. If I let myself go there, I become so full of rage that I actually wish Craig dead and scare the shit out of myself. So I don't let myself feel and I stay paralyzed. I can't see any way out of this. I don't know what the answer is. But I don't really want to talk about my feelings. My feelings are a black hole and if you take me in there, I'm afraid I'll never get out. I don't have that luxury because I'm a mother. I've got three kids and a career and I need to be strong and move forward, so I just need some practical advice. My question is this: I love my kids, I love my sister, and my parents, and my work. Is that enough? Can I just skip over this whole intimate relationship thing for the rest of my life? I just want to be a mom and write and go to bed alone forever. That's my dream. So, you know, statistically speaking, if I divorce Craig, what are the chances my future self will want to find someone else?"

Ann puts down her pen and notebook and looks at me for a long moment. Then she says, "It seems that people are made for intimacy. It's near impossible to avoid that instinct. I'd say your chances of eventually feeling drawn to someone else are extremely high."

"Damnit," I say. "So my future self is going to forget this mess and this pain and eventually want another relationship? All right. When this fool that is my future self meets somebody, what are the chances that my new relationship will be better than the shitty one I'm in now? Can you give me percentages?"

"Okay. Well, I don't know Craig yet, but let's start with this future relationship. Let's say you meet someone great in five years. Your relationship potential starts at a hundred percent. Take off ten percent for the inevitable tension that'll arise as he helps raise your kids. Take off another ten percent as you watch Craig marry someone else and you struggle to let her help raise your kids. Take off five percent because of second-marriage baggage, and another ten percent because divorce is so expensive that money will likely be an issue. Now take off another ten percent to account for this particular guy's quirks and hang-ups and imperfections. That's a fifty-five. Now take off another twenty percent if you bring all this pain into your next relationship. So you're at thirty-five percent. A low F."

I look back at Ann and feel surprised and grateful. She is

giving me *numbers* because she understands that in the midst of this chaos, numbers are what I need. She is not selling me any love bullshit. She is a woman giving it straight to another woman. This is just math to us. Ann's face says, *Look, I'm not saying it's right, I'm just saying this is what we've got to work with.* I am, in this moment, certain that Ann is on my team. I've only known her for ten minutes, but I trust her.

"Fantastic," I say. "I *have* that. I already have my very own F relationship. I mean, Craig is devastated and working hard to get me back, but we are still a solid F. No question about that."

"Yeah. The F you know, right? We have a lot to figure out. I'm just saying there's no easy escape here. Going will be tough and staying will be tough. It's going to be hard either way. We just have to figure out which hard is right for you."

"If I stay, then I need you to tell me how to be married and never have sex again. I'm done with sex. Such a cluster. I've been handing over my body to boys since I decided that I needed taller, stronger, more confident people to protect me and claim me and tell me I was important and beautiful. I can forgive my child self for that, but now that I'm a grown-up, haven't I earned the right to keep my own body to myself? Don't I have my own power now? Yes, I do. Still, our whole marriage, Craig can stop me anytime and say, 'I want something and I want it from you because you are here. So I am going to request that you stop what you are doing, strip down, and meet my wants. This will prove that you love me. That we love each other. That all is well.' He can say all of this with just one smile. And if I don't want to smile back and drop everything to meet his wants, I'm rejecting him. What if I'm just refusing to reject myself for once? Especially now, since I know it's not enough anyway? That he's been using other bodies just like he's been using mine? Forget it. Sex has done nothing but hurt me. It's a dangerous game rigged in their favor. I want to wash my hands of it. Whatever the hell kind of intimacy that is, I don't want it. I have intimacy. I have friendship. I have my kids. I have my sister and my writing and my dogs. I don't need sex. I really think I'm beyond sex. Above it maybe. I think I might be Gandhi."

"You're Gandhi? Tell me more."

"I don't like sex. Since everybody else I know claims to love it, I used to secretly wonder if I was a repressed gay person. But when I admitted this to a gay friend, she reminded me that gay people have sexual feelings for people of the same sex, not a lack of sexual feelings for anyone. So then I decided that I was asexual, or maybe a person who was supposed to be celibate for spiritual reasons, like Gandhi. I'd always suspected I was almost exactly like Gandhi. So what I'm saying is that if Craig and I end up together, he's going to need to channel Mrs. Gandhi and just deal. Obviously, this will be the least he can freaking do."

Ann nods and replies, "Yes, the only downside of being Gandhi is that while the kids are at school you'll need to start some kind of peaceful revolution and then maybe be murdered for it."

"That's fine. Not a problem. It's unfortunate, but it doesn't seem half as difficult as figuring out this sex thing. I accept that fate. I am totally willing to die for my cause of not making out."

"Glennon, I've only known you for a few minutes, but I'm pretty sure you're not Gandhi."

"Fine. I won't be Gandhi. I'll be Elsa from *Frozen*. I just want to be Elsa and live in an ice castle far away and sing anthems by myself and braid my hair and shoot ice out through my hands at men who try to visit."

"Ah, but Elsa had to come back—because no one can live a full life isolated from other people."

"Yes. She came back, I'll give you that. But I guarantee she didn't have to have any sex. She just got true love from her sister and kept busy being queen. And you better believe all the men stayed a little afraid of her forever. That's what I want."

Ann smiles. It is not a therapist smile, not a patronizing smile, not even a sympathetic smile. It's a smile of recognition. There is a twinkle in her eye that says, *Yep. I hear you, sister. I've got a little Elsa in me, too.* But I can see in her face that she doesn't believe the castle is the right place for me. Ann wants to help me thaw.

"Just real quick, you should probably know that I'm a recovering everything. I became bulimic when I was ten, and then an alcoholic. I got sober eleven years ago."

"Wow. What happened? Why do you think you became bulimic so young?"

"I don't know. Overachiever, I suppose. Ahead of my time. I don't want to talk about that either. It was another lifetime. When I found out I was pregnant I wrapped all that up in a box and put it away. I need to move forward. Let's just stick to the family stuff. I have small people to take care of now."

"Okay. It makes sense though. Many women who feel the way you do about sex have histories of body and eating struggles. I know you don't want to, but instead of setting aside your past and concentrating on Craig, we need to put Craig aside and concentrate on your past. Glennon, you both have work to do—separate and together—and the goal of the work is not necessarily reunification. The work is about you. You are going to have to learn to be intimate. If you box up your sexuality and put it in a closet, your life will never be as full as it could be. You're a smart woman. You know this is not all about Craig. This is an opportunity for you to figure some things out."

"Ah, yes. An Afgo."

"Excuse me?"

"Another fucking growth opportunity."

"Yes. An Afgo. In the meantime, let's decide what boundaries we need to put into place so you can feel safe in your home."

"I need Craig to move out of our room. I need him to not touch me."

She writes those things down. "Great, give this list to Craig and tell him it's what you need for now. Then let's figure out how to help you make peace with your body. We've got to host a reunion. Bring back together your body, mind, and spirit. Vote your body back on the island. Make you whole again."

"That sounds really hard. Do you have a pill for that?"

She smiles and starts filling out the paperwork. "No more pills. We have to do the work." Next to diagnosis, she's written a number. "What does that number mean?" I ask.

"It means 'adjustment disorder.'"

"Ah. What am I not adjusting to?"

Ann smiles. "Life, perhaps?"

"Yes. Well, how does one adjust to life? How does one adjust to something that won't ever stay the same? Anyway, it hasn't even been forty years yet. I just need some more time."

"You've got time. You've got all the time you need. One more thing. The way the brain works is this: We make a hypothesis about someone, and then our brain searches for information to verify our hypothesis. You've decided that Craig is a fool who is unworthy of you, and I don't blame you. But because of that belief, your brain is finding that information. You are actively making that true. Just as an experiment, what if—just for a week—you tried on the hypothesis that Craig is a deeply flawed but good man who loves you and is working hard to keep you? If you decide he's that man, you might find proof to back it up. And also when you feel the anxiety: Take three deep breaths. Then think. Don't think before you breathe."

"Okay," I say. I take three breaths, thank Ann, and walk out her door.

⁓

That evening, I look into my bedroom mirror until I don't recognize myself. It feels similar to staring at a familiar word so long that it seems all wrong, misspelled. I look into my own eyes, and that feels so overly intimate that my insides start to flutter. It feels almost aggressive, like I'm staring down a stranger. I reach out and touch the mirror. Who is that? Why is it so hard for me to believe that the figure I see is as much *me* as the mind trying to recognize her? I look away from the mirror, down at myself, and try to believe. I touch my legs and cross my arms, embracing myself. I try to notice that when I touch myself, I feel it. Why did I abandon this self of mine? Why does it feel like my whole life has been an out-of-body experience? I think back to something Ann asked me: "Glennon, what happened when you were ten?"

Ten is when I noticed that I was chubbier, frizzier, oilier than the other girls. I became self-conscious. My body started to feel like a separate, strange entity, and I thought it odd that people would examine and judge *me* based on what they saw, something that didn't have much to do with who I was. I just didn't feel like my body was at all a decent representation of me, but it was all I had to send out to the world. So I did what I had to do. I went out into the world. But being human always felt like too private an experience to share with other people. In public I felt naked, exposed, utterly vulnerable. And so I started hating my body. Not just the shape of it, although there was that. I hated having a body at all. My body made it impossible for me to succeed at being a girl. The universe had presented me with some very obvious rules for femaleness: Be small and quiet and wispy and stoic and light and smooth and don't fart or sweat or bleed or bloat or tire or hunger or yearn. But the universe had also already issued me this lumpy, loud, smelly, hungry, longing body—making it impossible to follow the rules. Being human in a world with no tolerance for humanity felt like a setup, a game I couldn't win. But instead of understanding that there might be something wrong with the world, I decided there was something wrong with me. I made a hypothesis about myself: I am damaged and broken. I should be shiny and happy and perfect and since I'm not, I should never expose myself. I should just find a safe hiding place. And so I retreated out of my body and out of the world, every chance I could.

My first escape was books. Oh, books! I lived for books. I took one everywhere I went. To the pool, to the babysitter's, to friends' houses in case things got awkward. I was constantly in a corner with my head down in a book—there but not there at all. Books are how I learned to disappear, to live in a world other than the uncomfortable physical one. And then I found bulimia, and heaven was both: a plate of food and a book. Then the food turned into booze and sex and drugs—one hiding place after another. And after I got sober, I became a writer. How predictable and convenient! A writer is a helicopter; she is not as much having a human experience as she is circling above human experience, reporting from a safe distance. Even if she visits the present moment, she's just there to gather material. I'd been gone since I was ten. Gone, gone, gone.

Earlier in the evening I was washing dishes and Amma walked into the kitchen. She was trying to get my attention but I didn't notice until she pulled on my leg and said, "Mommy, Mommy! Are you underwater again?" Underwater is what she calls it when I'm deep in thought. I'm like a submerged scuba diver, trying to search for treasure while people keep pulling at me, beckoning me back to the surface. I want to say, *Leave me alone! I am comfortable down here. I cannot pay attention to you, because I am too busy thinking about you.* I am either hovering above my life or diving deep beneath it.

I think about Craig and how I experience his need for affection as a constant interruption. How he is always insisting I resurface or land, and how much I resent it. The truth is that I've found my mind's life to be both safer and more interesting than my real life with him. When I'm lost in my thoughts, I am in the deep, underneath, where the treasure is. Life up there with him is, well, shallow.

But what if I've been wrong? What if what's real is out there, not in here? What if the purpose of life is connection, and what if you can only connect on the surface? Maybe the price of refusing to live in my body is loneliness.

I consider the question people ask me again and again when they hear the News: Glennon, are you in love with him? This question baffles and frustrates me. What do they mean? Do they even know what they mean? What the hell does *in love* mean? I'd always assumed that *in love* was some perfect storm of feelings that some couples were just lucky enough to have. But now I wonder, is love not a feeling but a place between two present people? A sacred place created when two people decide it's safe enough to let their real selves surface and touch each other? Is that why it's called *in* love? Because you have to visit there? And was I unable to grasp this concept because I was trying to understand it with my hovering mind—and love can't be known that way? Can the place *in love* only be experienced, traveled to? Maybe the cost of being a hoverer and a diver—someone who thinks about love and analyzes love and admires love from a distance—is that I cannot be *in love.* Because I don't go there. I stay removed. I have somehow decided that if I'm not truly present, I can't be hurt by people, but what if I can't be loved by them either? What if my body is the only vessel I have that can bring me to love?

Reunion. Ann was right—that's what I needed. Early in my life there had been a civil war, and my body had ceded from our union. How can I bring it back? I want a truce. I want to be whole. I want to learn to live in this body, in this world, with my people. I don't want to be trapped inside myself forever. I want to be in love.

I leave the mirror and walk to Tish's room. I curl up next to her while she sleeps, and hold her body close to mine. Her hair smells like coconut shampoo and fresh dirt. Her cheek feels like satin. Her breath on my arm is steady and warm. When I am with her, I am landed. I am loving her with all of my senses. I am in love, here, with her. I start to feel less frantic. I think of all the times my body has reached out to hold her, to feed her and hug her and dress her and bathe her and cradle her while she slept. My body has loved her and been loved by her. I must know how to visit love with my body. I must know. She wakes and I kiss her forehead and then I leave. She needs to sleep.

I climb back into my bed and wrap myself in the covers, tight, like a cocoon. I want to be here, in my body. With her. With the others. If love is a place, even if it's a scary place, I want to live there. As I fall asleep, I decide to stop writing for a long while. I need to live this, not create it. I need to let it be what it is, let it become—without forcing my pain into art. I need whatever happens with my family to be real, not shoved into a storyline. I will not try to control it by making sense of it. This is not material. This is my life. These people are not characters. I'll let go of control and live this instead of write it. I will not hide from this by hovering above or diving below. I'll land inside of it. My bedroom door opens and my dog, Theo, walks in, jumps onto my bed, and curls up in the nook behind my knees. I feel his warmth and the weight of his body grounding my legs, holding me down like an anchor. I'm in love with Theo right now, I think. I'm here, and he's here. We're together. But dogs and small children are one thing. It's easy to let myself fall into love with them because they can't hurt me. Grown-ups are another thing entirely. Grown-ups are dangerous. And yet. I want to fall in grown-up love. I want risky, true, scary love. I want to learn how to let my body bring me to love with an equal partner. I want that.

12

THE NEXT MORNING my writer-friend Mia calls. When I ask how she's doing, she says, "Marriage is good, kids are happy, not a problem in the world. It's terrible. I've got zero material. How's your shit show going, you lucky duck?" When I tell her about my need for reunion I expect her to laugh, but instead she says, "How about yoga? That's what they do there, you know. All that body, mind, spirit stuff. Why don't you go today?" I hang up the phone, sit in my kitchen, and stare at the wall. She's right. Yoga feels like the next right thing.

I drive to a nearby yoga studio and as soon as I walk into the lobby, the smell of incense hits me like proof God is there. I rent a mat, tiptoe into the yoga room, and wait. After a few minutes, the teacher walks in and introduces herself as Allison. Right away, Allison starts offering gentle, steady, specific directions about what to do with our bodies. Put your right hand here, tilt your head to the side, move your left leg there. I feel relieved, like I've been driving through treacherous conditions up a steep mountain and Allison has suddenly appeared to take the wheel. For months, I've been the decision maker, examining each possible move, then stepping lightly and stopping to measure the havoc each step may have wreaked upon my family. I've felt like the unqualified God of my family's future. But here, in this warm little room tucked away from my life, Allison is in charge. It feels like the goal here is to pretend for a while that I am not the God of my life. Or maybe to stop pretending that I've ever been the God of my life. All I know is that there is no move I can make in this little room that will hurt my children or me. I want to stay here forever, not making decisions, not thinking, not screwing anything up, concentrating only on where to put my hands and feet. I love not being God. I want to not be God forever, which is why my heart sinks when Allison bows to the God in us, says that class is over, and stops telling us what to do.

~

The next morning I'm back on my mat in the front row of the studio, excitedly waiting for the God in Allison to restore order to my world again. I go again the next morning, and then the next, and the next after that. I start learning in that room, but differently than I've ever learned before. In yoga, instead of using my mind to download wisdom, I use my body. Allison tells me to do something with my legs, "Settle into Warrior Two, stand firm, ground your legs and you won't fall; balance is created by equal forces pressing in on an object." I stand there, pressing my legs together, and it hits me: *Wait, what? I've been trying to find my balance by eliminating pressure from my life. The demands of work, friendship, and family all felt so heavy. But what if all this pressure isn't what's throwing me off, but what's holding me steady? What if pressure is just love and love is what keeps me anchored?* Complete shift. My body is teaching my mind.

Over and over in those classes, my body will do something new and Allison will say something new, and I will suddenly understand something I've never understood before. It is a stunning revelation: My body can be a teacher, a conduit of wisdom. It still feels like my body is a separate entity, but I'm growing to respect it. My body is a new witty friend I'm beginning to eye with curiosity. *What is going on with you?* I ask it. *Are you smarter than I gave you credit for?* I knew I was put on the earth to love and to learn. I knew that. I just didn't know I needed my body to do both.

Just as I learn to trust my body, I start losing faith in my mind. It seems fair to me that the harder I work, the more progress I should make. I'm desperate to pay whatever dues will earn me my peace, stability, and life back. So I continue with yoga, meet with Ann regularly, carve out my daily quiet time. I do everything a grieving person is supposed to do to climb out. Sometimes I feel strength and hope that last hours. Bundled in that hope, I feel confident enough to plan an outing with the kids or to go grocery shopping. Then, out of nowhere, while I'm at the playground or walking down the cereal aisle, hopelessness appears in front me, staring me down like a snarling dog. I freeze, knowing that if I run, it'll catch me. There is no way to overpower, outrun, or outsmart the mad dog of hopelessness because it's simply more vicious than I. The only thing to do is let it attack, go limp in its jaws, and be shaken. But I notice one promising pattern. If I play dead, it will eventually let me go. I start thinking of the dog of hopelessness as an obstacle that will reappear on every curve of the spiral staircase. He'll always be there waiting and snarling, but with every go-round, I'll be more confident and less fearful. Eventually, I'll learn the tricks that will allow me to breeze right past him. But the mad dog of hopelessness will always be there. My spiral staircase of progress means that my pain will be both behind me and in front of me, every damn day. I'll never be "over it," but I vow to be stronger each time I face it. Maybe the pain won't change, but I will. I keep climbing.

~

Three months after I start yoga and therapy, I'm in the kitchen, pouring the kids' cereal while they rub their sleepy eyes and try to wake up. Craig has started seeing Ann both with me and on his own. It's a positive development, but we're still sleeping in separate bedrooms and the kids are struggling to understand. Craig walks out of his bedroom and the kids watch him approach the table. We try to smile at each other to ease the awkwardness but there is no ignoring the heaviness of the moment. When I put the spoons on the table, Craig touches my hand and I recoil. The kids witness this, and Chase and Tish look away quickly. But Amma is still too young and too honest to pretend, so she starts to cry. I sit down on her chair, pull her into my lap, and hold her like a baby. I pat her hair and say, "It's okay, honey, everything's okay. We're fine, baby. We're fine." I say this over and over again, like I'm trying to cast a spell. I'm lying. Nothing is okay. I look into Amma's eyes and find proof that she doesn't believe me. She knows better now. She is four and she already knows that I can't make it all better.

As I hold her and avoid eye contact with the rest of the family, I feel nothing but failure. This is the one thing I promised myself I'd get right. I'd let them be kids by protecting their hearts from pain. I've failed. Their hearts are broken. I wipe Amma's tears and see that Craig has turned toward the sink. He is pretending to wash dishes so the kids won't see his tears. Chase pushes away his cereal and walks over to me. He wraps his arms around my shoulders. "It's okay, Mama," he whispers. *Oh, God. He's nine, and he feels like he needs to comfort me. By pretending. Failure. Failure, Glennon.* The ache of the moment becomes too much to bear. I have to get us out of this. I shake my head back and forth, wipe my eyes, steel my heart, smile, and say, "Okay, guys. Let's get moving. We're fine! Go get dressed for school."

Everybody leaves their breakfasts and disappears into their own rooms. I watch them and think, *We were there. We were inside love, being real, together—and I just pushed us all out, back into our little rooms, back into our own scared, safe, alone selves. Double failure.*

~

After I drop the kids off at school, all I want to do is go back home and crawl into bed. I can't though, because Craig is there and I don't want to face him. So I drive to the yoga studio. I walk into the lobby and the receptionist tells me that Allison's class is full. I want to throw myself on the floor in front of her and yell *No! I need Allison! This is the last straw!* But it dawns on me that throwing a fit would be a waste of time. There is no promise that straws will be distributed fairly. *This is the last straw!* Ha! According to whom? My mind is a toddler throwing pointless tantrums, wasting all our energy, getting us nowhere. Instead of declaring to the world that I have too many straws, I must get strong enough to carry all the straws I've got. So I bring my mat and all my invisible damn straws into a different yoga class and sit down.

As I'm setting up, I note that the air-conditioning must be broken because it's at least one hundred degrees in the room. Even so, all the other students in the class are sitting cross-legged and smiling, so I try to join them in their Zen attitudes of detachment. But the hotter it gets, the sweatier and angrier I become. I am attached to air-conditioning. Very attached. After three minutes of sweating, I decide that since I am not even a real Buddhist, it is fine to be pissed about this. So I huff and puff and start gathering my things to leave. But as soon as I stand up, our teacher walks into the room. She closes the door behind her and says, "Hello. I'm Amy. Thank you for coming to hot yoga."

Hot yoga? What fresh hell is this? Too embarrassed to leave, I sit back down, wipe sweat from my face, and stare at the door longingly as the room starts closing in on me. While I scramble to plot my escape, Amy says, "Let's decide on our intentions for class." She nods to a woman up front who smiles and says, "My intention is to embrace loving-kindness today." The second person says, "I want to radiate sunlight to all creation." I sit, incredulous, as the next few ask for peace, strength, and clarity. *What the hell are these people talking about? What am I doing wasting my time in here when my entire life is falling apart out there? Loving-kindness? I have real problems, people!* Then it's my turn and Amy is looking right at me. When I open my mouth, this is what comes out: "My intention is just to stay on this mat and make it through whatever is about to happen without running out of here." My voice trembles, and the room gets very quiet. Something about Amy's eyes makes it clear to me that I've just said something important.

Amy breaks the silence by replying, "Yes. You just be still on your mat. Yes."

She starts the class, and for ninety minutes I sit still on my mat with no escape from my self. It is torturous. All the images I've been trying to outrun appear in front of me. Ghosts from the past: There I am on the laundry room floor; there is my baby crying into her cereal; there is Craig taking another woman to bed; and there they are afterward, hugging, kissing, laughing. Ghosts from the future: There is Craig walking down the aisle with another woman; there is Tish as a flower girl—wait, is that bride stopping to tuck my little girl's hair behind her ear? Is she holding my girl's hand? No, No, NO! It's like a sadistic game of Whac-A-Mole in which the moles are my worst fears popping up in front of me and I have no mallet. I have nothing to swat at these ghosts with, no way to distract myself from them, nowhere to run from them, nothing to do at all but be still and face them. I wipe away tears that keep forming in response to my misery and the restlessness that feels like it might actually kill me. Sitting there, unmoving, my body hurts as much as my heart does. I feel so *alone* with my love and pain.

As I watch the others—people who are not just sitting, but stretching, and posing, and contorting—I consider feeling embarrassed. I try to remember that their intentions are not my intentions, their straws are not my straws, their paths are not my path. My directions were specific and personal: Be still and do not run out of here. A few times I choke back loud tears and I feel embarrassed again. All I can do is let myself feel embarrassed. *Let them hear you. We are all here for different things. You are here to learn how to stay on your mat and feel the pain without running out of here. Be still.* So the images keep coming and I just let my tears fall and mix into my sweat. I let it all be terrifying and horrible and unfair. I sit there and accept how unacceptable it all is. I just let it be.

Somehow, Amy understands. She comes by my mat to check on me throughout the class, and on her face I see respect. She knows I'm learning something important. I can tell she's already learned it. Many times, maybe. Every few minutes she looks at me and gives a little nod that means, Yes, you're doing this right. Don't give up. Don't run out. And finally, after ninety minutes, we are done. Amy asks us to lie down, and I lower myself to the floor and open my eyes to the ceiling. I realize that I have allowed myself to see it all and feel it all and I have survived. All the ghosts are still there, but they're less threatening now. They can scare me, but they cannot kill me. They tried, but I won. Everything is still a bloody mess, yet here I am. Alive. I'd been fully human for an hour and a half and it had hurt like hell. It had almost killed me, but not quite. That *not quite* part seems incredibly important.

I close my eyes and when the tears flow downward toward my mat, I feel surprised that there's any liquid left inside of me. Then I feel a hand on my arm, and along with it, an immediate twinge of shame: I am sweaty and crying and snotty and gross and someone is close to me. Up close, touching me. But I do not pull away. I do not wipe my eyes or my nose. I just let us be. I open my eyes and Amy is right there next to me and she says, "That—what you just did? That is the Journey of the Warrior. Now, don't forget to breathe. You need to remember to breathe." I do not understand why everyone keeps telling me to breathe. I'm alive, aren't I? Isn't it clear that I'm breathing? And what is the Journey of the Warrior?

Finally Amy bows to us and tells us that the God in her honors the God in us. She opens the door and the cool air rushes in. I walk out through the lobby and into the sun and experience an overwhelming sense of déjà vu. *The Journey of the Warrior.* This phrase rings a bell in my soul, but why? I climb into my van, rush home, and pull Pema Chödrön's *When Things Fall Apart* off my nightstand. I flip to a page I've dog-eared and I run my finger down the lines to a sentence I'd underlined and highlighted but hadn't really understood until now:

> So even if the hot loneliness is there, and for 1.6 seconds we sit with that restlessness when yesterday we couldn't sit for even one, that's the journey of the warrior.

I sit down on the floor and as I read that sentence over and over, I understand that my entire life has been a race from the hot loneliness. I picture ten-year-old me, feeling my anger, fear, jealousy, otherness, unbelonging for the first time and understanding these uncomfortable but normal human feelings to be wrong, shameful. I thought I needed to hide these feelings, escape them, fix them, deliver myself from them. I didn't know that everyone feels the hot loneliness. I didn't know that it would pass. So for the next twenty years, every time anger or fear or loneliness started bubbling up, I reached for an easy button—a book, a binge, a beer, a body, a shopping spree, a Facebook feed—to shove it back down. I'd press that button and find myself magically transported to a pain-free place. Distracted, numbed, underwater, gone. Off my mat again and again. Running out of here.

Oh my God—what if the transporting is keeping me from transformation? What if my anger, my fear, my loneliness were never mistakes, but invitations? What if in skipping the pain, I was missing my lessons? Instead of running away from my pain, was I supposed to run toward it? Perhaps pain was not a hot potato after all, but a traveling professor. Maybe instead of slamming the door on pain, I need to throw open the door wide and say, Come in. Sit down with me. And don't leave until you've taught me what I need to know.

I've never let myself trust love because I've never let myself trust pain. What if pain—like love—is just a place brave people visit? What if both require presence, staying on your mat, and being still? If this is true, then maybe instead of resisting the pain, I need to resist the easy buttons. Maybe my reliance on numbing is keeping me from the two things I was born for: learning and loving. I could go on hitting easy buttons until I die and feel no pain, but the cost of that decision could be that I'll never learn, love, or be truly alive.

I started numbing with food at age ten. Through our therapy sessions, I learned that Craig started numbing with porn when he was just a few years older. Porn was his relief, his underneath, his easy button. He told me he'd hide in his room, watching smuggled videos, first feeling relief, and then feeling ashamed—just like I felt during and after a binge. Maybe Craig was becoming aware of his hot loneliness, too, and porn was how he learned to jump off his mat. Like me, he would've had no way of knowing that his restlessness was just human. Just as I'd understood the rules for girls, surely he'd absorbed the world's rules for boys—that emotions are forbidden, that to be a successful boy he needed to "buck up and be a man." Do girls abandon our bodies because that's where we're shamed and boys abandon their emotions because that's where they're shamed? *Little boys: Don't feel. Little girls: Don't hunger.*

I picture both of our ten-year-old selves: I am in the corner reading, while Craig is on the soccer field playing. All day, every day, he played soccer. And then, left with his feelings in the stillness, there was porn. And as he grew, there were women's bodies. Body-to-body is how he felt known, seen, loved. And then he became a model, continuing to build his identity with his body. His whole life has been a retreat into his body. My whole life has been a retreat into my mind. Is this why it is so hard for us to love each other? Because he understands love to be the joining of two bodies, and I believe love to be the joining of two minds? Neither of us is bringing our whole self to the other. Maybe we are exiled from each other because we are each exiled from a part of ourselves.

Most of the messages we receive every day are from people selling easy buttons. Marketers need us to believe that our pain is a mistake that can be solved with their product. And so they ask, *Feel lonely? Feel sad? Life hard? Well that's certainly not because life can be lonely and sad and hard, so everybody feels that way. No, it's because you don't have this toy, these jeans, this hair, these countertops, this ice cream, this booze, this woman . . . fix your hot loneliness with THIS.* So we consume and consume but it never works, because you can never get enough of what you don't need. The world tells us a story about our hot loneliness so that we'll buy their easy buttons forever. We accept this story as truth because we don't realize that their story is the poison in our air. Our pain is not the poison; the lies about the pain are.

Craig and I have spent our lives breathing the same poisonous air. Along the way, we've internalized the lies: *You are supposed to be happy all the time. Everybody else is! Avoid the pain! You don't need it, it's not meant for you. Just push this button.* Finally, I was being quiet and still enough to hear the truth: *You are not supposed to be happy all the time. Life hurts and it's hard. Not because you're doing it wrong, but because it hurts for everybody. Don't avoid the pain. You need it. It's meant for you. Be still with it, let it come, let it go, let it leave you with the fuel you'll burn to get your work done on this earth.*

There on the floor, I know the truth. We either allow ourselves to feel the burn of our own pain or someone we love gets burned by it. Craig and I had spent our lives denying our pain, but that did not make it disappear. Since we refused to hold it, we passed it on to the people we loved. Since I refused to feel my pain, I passed it on to my parents and my sister. Since Craig refused to feel his, my kids and I were carrying it. But maybe Craig hadn't meant to pass his pain on to me. Maybe he hadn't meant to hurt me with those other women any more than I'd meant to hurt my family with booze. We were each just reaching for the easy buttons we learned to use long before we even met.

My mind flashes to Amma's tears at breakfast. That very morning, she was trying to feel her hot loneliness and I'd grabbed it from her. "It's okay. We're fine, baby. We're fine," I'd said. I'd pulled out the easy buttons of pretending and denial and held them out to her. I'd encouraged her to jump off her mat. I'd reacted this way because I feared that my baby's pain was my failure. But if learning to sit with hot loneliness is my warrior journey, isn't it hers, too? More than anything, I want Amma to grow to be a brave, kind, wise, resilient woman. So what is it in a human life that creates bravery, kindness, wisdom, and resilience? What if it's pain? What if it's the struggle? What if I was trying to take from Amma the one thing that would make her the woman I dreamed she'd become? The bravest people I know are those who've walked through the fire and come out on the other side. They are those who've overcome, not those who've had nothing to overcome. Maybe my job as Amma's mother is not to protect her from pain, but to hold her hand and walk into it with her. Perhaps the wisdom she needs for her journey is not only inside of me: It's also inside her struggle. If I want to invite Amma to begin the Journey of the Warrior, I need to stop distracting her from her hot loneliness. I need to look at her and say, "I see your pain. It's real. I feel it, too. We can handle it, baby. We can do hard things. Because we are Warriors."

Just as these new understandings about Craig and Amma settle, my thoughts shift to my friends. I'd been so angry with them for grabbing my pain from me in the wake of the News. But maybe my friends were loving me the best way they knew how, just like I was trying to love Amma. We think our job as humans is to avoid pain, our job as parents is to protect our children from pain, and our job as friends is to fix each other's pain. Maybe that's why we all feel like failures so often—because we all have the wrong job description for love. What my friends didn't know about me and I didn't know about Amma is that people who are hurting don't need Avoiders, Protectors, or Fixers. What we need are patient, loving witnesses. People to sit quietly and hold space for us. People to stand in helpless vigil to our pain.

There on the floor, I promise myself that I'll be that kind of mother, that kind of friend. I'll show up and stand humble in the face of a loved one's pain. I'll admit I'm as empty-handed, dumbstruck, and out of ideas as she is. I won't try to make sense of things or require more than she can offer. I won't let my discomfort with her pain keep me from witnessing it for her. I'll never try to grab or fix her pain, because I know that for as long as it takes, her pain will also be her comfort. It will be all she has left. Grief is love's souvenir. It's our proof that we once loved. Grief is the receipt we wave in the air that says to the world: *Look! Love was once mine. I loved well. Here is my proof that I paid the price.* So I'll just show up and sit quietly and practice not being God with her. *I'm so sorry,* I'll say. *Thank you for trusting me enough to invite me close. I see your pain and it's real. I'm so sorry.*

The Journey of the Warrior. This is it. The journey is learning that pain, like love, is simply something to surrender to. It's a holy space we can enter with people only if we promise not to tidy up. So I will sit with my pain by letting my own heart break. I will love others in pain by volunteering to let my heart break with theirs. I'll be helpless and broken and still—surrendered to my powerlessness. Mutual surrender, maybe that's an act of love. Surrendering to this thing that's bigger than we are: this love, this pain. The courage to surrender comes from knowing that the love and pain will almost kill us, but not quite.

~

Holding Chödrön's book to my heart, I lean back against my bedroom wall, exhausted. My body has done its work. My body is my teacher now, and I have learned. Pain and love are places I must be brave enough to visit. My courage will come from knowing I can handle whatever I encounter there—because I was designed by my creator to not only survive pain and love but also to become whole inside it. I was born to do this. I am a Warrior.

Suddenly I feel deeply hungry. I don't hear anyone in the house, so I walk woozily to the kitchen. Craig is there. He looks at me and seems surprised. I'm soaking wet and red from tears and sweat. I look at him and say, "I'm so hungry." I sound weaker and more desperate than I'd planned.

Craig's eyes widen and he says, "Really? Let me make you something. Can I make you some real food?" Now his voice sounds excited, almost frantic.

When I got sober, I quit bingeing and purging, but I never really learned to feed myself. A lifetime of bingeing was enough to prove to me that my appetite was animalistic and shameful. It was not to be trusted, so I locked it away. I treated my hunger like a prisoner. I doled out daily rations of food-like products—tiny portions of bars, shakes, juices, leftovers—anything that would get me by without awaking my inner glutton. *Little girl: Don't hunger.* I decided about food the same thing fundamentalists decide about religion: Enough rules will keep us safe from ourselves. But suddenly I want to feed myself, and Craig wants to feed me. I am starting to feel real and I need real food. So I say, "Yes, please."

Craig goes to the refrigerator and I follow, and even though it is only eleven in the morning, we work side by side making cheeseburgers, baked potatoes, and salad. The smell of the burgers fills the kitchen and once, when I reach over, Craig touches my hand. I do not pull away. Not right away, at least. When we're done preparing the meal, Craig takes my plate and fills it to the edges.

We sit down at the table and Craig says grace: "Help our family please, Amen." I look at my plate and feel overwhelmed. There are no directions here, no clear-cut boundaries, no single servings, no wrappers, no scoop to measure what is okay for me to have and what is too much. Nothing to protect me from my appetite. How will I know where to start or when to stop? I look over at Craig and see that he is already eating. How is this so easy for him?

I look at my salad and think, *I should start there,* but then I see the burger and it suddenly seems imperative that I ignore the should of my mind and respond instead to the want of my body. I pick up my burger and sink my teeth into it. Some of it crumbles and a river of juices and ketchup runs down my hand. I don't want to lose any of it, so I lick it off. Then I take another bite and chew and it feels like some sort of heaven; it feels like loving myself. And then the panicky feeling arises inside of me, but I tell myself to resist the urges to push the burger away or to swallow it whole. I can go slow and enjoy this. No one is going to take it from me. This plate is mine and I am allowed to have it all. I take another bite and sigh from the juicy joy. If I get too full, I can just be still. Fullness will pass, and I will survive.

Then I notice Craig watching me. He is witnessing my hunger, my burger ecstasy. I feel ridiculous, guilty, like I've been caught breaking the rules. But Craig is smiling. There is no scorn in his eyes, just a mixture of joy and relief. He is looking at me like he's wondering where I've been. I tell myself, *It's okay for a woman to hunger, Glennon. It's okay for her to satisfy her appetite, to enjoy all the juiciness. Remember, don't be a lady—be a Warrior. The Warrior feeds all three of her selves: mind, spirit, body.* I breathe deeply and then start on the potatoes. *Eat until you're full. Trust your body to guide you. Treat yourself like someone you love, Glennon. Listen to what you want and need and give it to yourself. Be your own friend.*

~

Later that night, after the kids are tucked in, I pass Craig. He's sitting at the kitchen table, staring at his hands. He looks nervous. He says, "Would you mind if we practiced talking?"

I say, "What? Practice *talking*?"

"Yeah. I know it sounds weird, but it's really hard for me to listen and respond right. You're good at conversation, so every time you want to talk, I feel afraid that I'm going to say the wrong thing. That's why I zone out. Ann says it's a fight-or-flight thing. I think this is why I forget what you've said sometimes, because I'm not really there. I just assumed I couldn't do it. Ann just thinks I'm out of practice, though. It's weird, I know. She said I should practice talking and listening."

I sit down in a chair on the other side of the table. "Not weird," I say. "I get it. Sometimes I feel that way when I'm touched. Threatened, I guess, so I just check out. I've been practicing staying in my body. That's what all the yoga is about. I think eating is a part of it, too. I always thought my body was broken. But maybe not. Maybe I'm just out of practice, too."

Craig sits still for a moment and then says quietly, "I love you. I want to know you. I know the way to you is through your mind. I'm trying to learn how to get there."

There is plenty of silence before I reply. "If you've never gotten to me, how do you know you love me?"

"I want to love you. I want to know you so I can love you well. I need you, but I want to love you, too."

"I get that, too. I do. I have to learn to use my body to reach you and you have to learn to use your mind to reach me. It's like 'The Gift of the Magi' or something."

Craig looks blank. "The what?"

"'The Gift of the Magi.'"

"What's that? Wait. Hold on." Craig pushes his chair back and disappears into the kitchen. He returns with a notebook and a pen. He sits down and starts writing.

"What are you doing?" I ask.

"I need to take notes. Ann suggested it. I know this is easy for you, but it's not for me. I think I'm going to have to write things down for a while. To remember."

I'd watched Craig feed his body and I'd marveled at how easy it was for him. *Right,* I think, *I'm learning to feed my body. He's learning to feed his mind.* So since he fed me, I feed him. I tell him the story of "The Gift of the Magi." It is the story of a couple with so little money and so much love that she sells her beautiful hair so she can buy him a watch chain and he sells his prized pocket watch so he can buy hair combs for her. They each sacrifice the object in which their identity is wrapped and they are left with nothing remaining to prove their worth to the world. But they have proved their worth to one another. They are lovers of each other, and that identity is truer than was her beauty or his status. They are left with the truth and the truth is love.

After the story Craig turns to a fresh page in his notebook. He says, "I know you're tired, but can you please tell me a story from when you were little?" So I tell him about Miracle. I tell the story I've told many times before, but he hears it for the first time. He leans forward with his body, asks questions, makes eye contact that is so intense and steady I have to look away again and again. Twice, we laugh, together. It's real, spontaneous laughter and it moves the air around us—the air that has grown so stale—and I wish the kids were awake to hear it. It sounds like hope. And I understand that shared laughter is sacred because it's proof that two people are right there at their surfaces with each other—they've come up for air together; neither has sunk away inside herself—both are right there, trying to touch. As we laugh I think, *Is this space we're in right now love? Are we in love right now? Can you only be in love with someone as often as you are fully present? How did we get here? Is it safe for me here?*

I look at the clock and it's midnight. Craig sees me notice the time and he says, "Go to sleep. You need to take care of yourself. I'll clean up." And I look down at my body and think, *Yes, this is my self. I need to take care of her.*

I look at Craig and say, "Thank you." I walk to my room, climb under the sheets, and fall asleep.

13

I WAKE UP, and since the sun is already streaming into my room, I know I've overslept. *Damnit, the kids will be late for school.* I stumble out of my room and into the kitchen, which is filled with the smells of breakfast. I'm grateful to see that the kids are already dressed for school and waiting at the table. Craig points to a plate and I sit down. He puts an omelet on the plate in front of me. I consider waving it away. I'd just eaten last night, after all. But then I notice the girls watching me. I check in with myself. My body wants the omelet, so I eat it. Then I eat two slices of toast and I drink a glass of orange juice and I feel ecstatic again, like I'm participating in a family celebration that's been happening right under my nose, three times a day. I've been missing it all this time. I clear the plates and Craig says he'll handle carpool. I kiss the kids goodbye, finish the dishes, sit back at the table, and wonder what to do with myself. Writing is still off limits, there's three more days until therapy, and I cannot handle any more yoga for a while. What next? I sit and consider what Ann, Allison, and Amy have all said to me: "You need to breathe, Glennon. Don't forget to breathe." Every time I hear this *breathe* advice, I roll my eyes. *I know how to breathe,* I think. But then I remember that I just learned how to eat yesterday. I remind myself I'm starting over. I'm unbecoming.

I walk over to my computer and enter: "Naples, Florida, breathing" into the search browser. I click on a link and I'm taken to a page about teaching the use of breath as a healing tool. *You've got to be kidding,* I think. I look closely and see that a class is being held five miles from my house, in the very same building where Craig delivered the News. The next step on my path lights up in front of me.

~

A few nights later, I find myself in a carpeted lobby surrounded by other people who apparently don't know how to breathe either. Soft meditative music is playing and there's a water feature running in each corner. The walls are covered with pictures of caterpillars turning into butterflies and quotes about caterpillars turning into butterflies and shelves display several statues of caterpillars turning into butterflies. It's warm and cocoon-like in here, and I'm grateful for it; I feel cozy and safe. Our breathing teacher sits cross-legged up front. Her name is Liz. Liz has long hair and she's wearing a T-shirt and jeans with a beaded necklace and no makeup. She tells us to roll out our mats and lie down. There are quite a few of us in this small room; we're close enough to hear each other's breath and smell each other's smells. Liz asks us to begin breathing deeply.

While we're lying and breathing, Liz starts talking about God. At least I think she's talking about God, but it's hard to tell at first because she keeps calling God "Source" and "Spirit." She tells us we can call God whatever we want, but she chooses Source because God is where we came from, and Spirit because it means breath, and God is always as close as our breath. She says that even though we're broken off from our source, we yearn to return—and we can return, simply by breathing. Liz laughs and says, "There are many institutions that don't want you to know that all you have to do to be with God is breathe, because then everybody'd quit jumping through their hoops. Breathing is free, you know. Knowing is important. You have to be still to know."

I open one eye to peek at the others. Are we allowed to talk like this? I feel thrilled and nervous, like we're in the back room of a high school party and somebody just pulled out the weed. Like we're holed up printing our own money instead of waiting in line at the bank. I look over at the door and half expect a cop or minister to bust in and break up our little Underground Ragamuffin God Group before we have time to plan a coup. I remember what the God Rep said to me about my separation: *Make sure you stay inside God's umbrella of protection, Glennon.* I am certain that this room is outside her umbrella. So why do I feel so tingly and alive?

You can call God whatever you want . . . can you really? This is not what I've been taught. I've been taught that I must call God a certain name or He will burn me forever. But Liz's idea is making me consider that Chase calls me Mom, Tish calls me Mommy, and

Amma calls me Mama. I've never wanted to burn them about it. I knew they were each talking to me. It seems logical to assume that the creator of the universe might be at least as mature as I am about this name issue.

I tune back into Liz's voice and she says, "Okay, now drop your breath. Start to breathe from your belly." She puts her hand on her stomach and says, "Watch your hand rise and fall with your breath." I try, but I can't do it. My chest is still rising while my stomach stays still. I am starting to get wheezy and panicky. Liz hears me struggling and sits down next to me. She places her hand on top of mine and says, "Down here, not from your chest. Go deeper. When we breathe from our chest, we live too high and we feel ungrounded. Go deep. Breathe low and live down here." I try again. Liz stays by my side with her hand on my belly for so long that I start to feel ashamed. I want to quit but I tell myself, *Be still. Stay on your mat. Follow her directions. Do not run out of here.* Eventually, I feel a shift. I'm in my belly now. I hear Liz say, "Well done."

What happens next lasts for one moment and forever. I feel myself begin to float up and out of the room, into a night sky filled with stars. As I rise, my chest opens and expands until I lose all my boundaries and I can no longer tell where I end and the sky begins. The eyes I'm using to see are the eyes of the sky. I'm huge, endless, infinite. For the first time in my life, I feel the utter absence of fear. I am completely comfortable. I am at peace. And I understand that I am in the middle of a reunion with God. This is a returning of my soul to its source. My soul's source is God, and God is love. I am, right at this moment, in perfect love with God and there is no fear in perfect love. Is this what they mean by eternity? It must be. This is the end. The end is the beginning. A returning to perfect love. Reunion for the soul. Why had I been taught to be afraid of God if In God is the one place in which fear does not exist? I feel in awe of this God, this love—I am awed but not afraid. Fear is not possible here. Fear and God together will never make sense to me again. I am loved and have always been loved and will always, always be loved. I have never been separated from this love, I have only convinced myself I was. I think of the woman who warned me not to step outside of God's protection and I want to go back and reassure her, "Sister, who needs an umbrella when you are the whole sky?"

All the way from the sky, I hear Liz ask us to slow our breathing and to land. I shift my breathing back to my chest and feel myself return to my body, like my soul is slipping back into its sleeping bag. I sit up slowly and look at the clock. An hour and a half has passed, which makes no sense at all. I notice that everyone is smiling shyly at each other. We started as strangers but we feel close now, like we've been on a strange, unsanctioned trip together. Liz asks if anyone wants to share about her experience. It's quiet until the woman beside me starts crying. She says, "I'm a pastor. I've been praying for twenty years and meditating for ten, trying to experience God. But I've never . . . I can't describe it. It was like . . . I am forgiven. I am beautiful and loved. I've been trying so hard to be better, different. But I am perfectly loved. Just as I am. I just . . . I never understood until now." I look at her and feel relieved. I haven't imagined this. She'd been the sky, too. I nod in solidarity with her and reach over to touch her arm. She puts her hand over mine to keep it there. I think of my dog, Theo, and how I need his weight on my legs each night like an anchor. I wonder if we need to be touched to come back to our bodies, to prove to ourselves that we exist, that we're real, that we've landed.

Just as I am, she'd said. *I'm loved just as I am.* She sounded so surprised. Me, too. It strikes me that it's always religious people who are most surprised by grace. Those hoops we become so exhausted from jumping through? We created them. We forget that our maker made us human, and so it's okay—maybe exactly right—to be human. We are ashamed of the design of the one we claim to worship. So we sweep up our mess and hide our doubts, contradictions, anger, and fear before showing ourselves to God, which is like putting on a fancy dress and makeup to prepare for an X-ray. I think about how the people who seem closest to God are often not dressed up and sitting in pews, but dressed down and sitting in folding chairs in recovery meetings. They have refused to cover themselves up any longer. They are the ones who are no longer pretending. They are the ones who know. Pain led them to their rock bottom, and rock bottom is the beginning of any honest life, any spiritual journey. These are the ones who know that faith is standing naked before your maker and asking what Craig asked me in the therapist's office that day: *I just need to know if you can really know me and still love me.* God's yes to us is free and final. Our yeses to each other are harder to come by.

I am not God, and yet Craig asked me that question. Since he'd asked me, I am the only one who can answer him. How will I answer? I think, *Is perfect love true or isn't it?* It seems to be a yes or no question. I wonder if Craig is not so much asking "Can you forgive me, Glennon?" as much as he's wondering, *Can God forgive me, Glennon?* Maybe before he needs to know if I can love him, he needs to know if he is worthy of love. I remember sitting on my parents' couch and wondering if I was worthy of love. I remember entering that little church and wondering if I was worthy of love. I remember. And I remember that Mary and my parents had answered me: *Yes*. Then the Gulf of Mexico had answered me: *Yes*. Tonight the sky had answered me yet again: *Yes, Yes, Yes*. In the face of that sky, the only true answer is: *Yes*. The truth is grace and grace makes no exceptions. I am not what I've done. And if I claim that as true, then I must also claim as true that Craig is not what he has done. I will need to say to him, *You are not what you've done. You are loved and have always been loved and will always be loved. And not only are you loved, but you are love. I don't know if I'll stay, I don't know if I'll trust you again, but I can tell you the truth when you've forgotten. I can be love's impartial witness for you. Love is what you're made of and grace is free for all. Grace and worthiness are yours for the taking.*

Grace makes no disclaimer. It's true for all or none. The price of grace for me is grace for Craig. But as soon as I consider grace for Craig, images start filling my mind like I'm a piggy bank and someone is making deposits. The deposits are images of women's faces, symbols of those Craig has slept with over the years. So, love seems to be asking, *If grace is true for you, and if it's true for Craig, is it true for them, too?* And that's when I understand that grace is a beautiful, terrible thing. That the price of love is high indeed. That for me, the price is this: I must stop pretending that I am any different from Craig and those women. My unforgiveness is just another easy button. We aren't different. We are exactly the same. We are individual pieces of a scattered puzzle and we are just a little lost down here. We are all desperate for reunion and we are trying to find it in all the wrong places. We use bodies and drugs and food to try to end our loneliness, because we don't understand that we're lonely down here because we are supposed to be lonely. Because we're in pieces. To be human is to be incomplete and constantly yearning for reunion. Some reunions just require a long, kind patience.

I think of Mary years ago, beckoning me to walk toward her. *Come. Right here. Right to me, Glennon. Just as you are.*

But, Mary, I'm young and afraid and unmarried and pregnant and lost and alone.

And she had said, *Me, too. God loves us this way. Come.*

If I want to bring all of myself to God, I will have to insist that others can, too. If I want to reside in God's open arms, if I want to refuse to be dismissed to the back office with the administrators, then I cannot send anyone else there. Our redemption is only as real as it is free. Grace can only be personal if it's also universal. My freedom and everyone else's is either bound or loosed together. Our only hope to be fully human together is to first insist upon our right to be fully human before God. And it will only be the acceptance that I am already loved perfectly by God that will let me forgive Craig and those women for loving so imperfectly. So I decide to give away what I need. *I'll pay the price of grace. Yes, grace is true for all of us. I choose all: myself and Craig and the other women—all of us.* And for the second time in only a few days, I find myself crying in a room full of strangers. I feel saved.

But even as I feel the weight of the world lifting, I know this peace won't last. I'll have to leave this room. I'll feel lost again. Fear and anger and panic will cover this grace and truth, just as clouds cover the stars. But fear doesn't make perfect love untrue any more than passing clouds make the stars untrue. I know how to find my way back to truth, to love, to peace, to God again. All I have to do is be still and breathe and wait for the clouds and fear to pass. Now the room has started feeling too small to hold all the love in my chest. I pick up my mat and walk out.

I drive home and walk into the house. I sit down next to Craig on the couch and he turns off the TV and looks at me nervously. I say, "Listen. Something weird happened to me tonight. I learned that we're the same, you and me. You thought sex was love and I thought booze and food were love and we got really lost. But that doesn't mean we're not loved. We are. You are. You're forgiven and you always were and you're loved—just as you are. It's all going to be okay. I think somehow it already is." Craig's eyes looks painfully hopeful, so I add, "Wait. This forgiveness, it's not personal yet. It doesn't mean I've forgiven you. I'm not there. I just know the truth is that you are forgiven. That whoever made you knows you, loves you, and isn't mad at you. And that whether we end up together or apart, we'll be okay. You, me, the kids—we're going to be fine. Nobody wants to punish us. We're totally, completely safe. The end of whatever road we choose will be redemption—love will win either way."

Craig is quiet as he thinks about this. I look at him and I can tell he's really listening—trying to take it in. "Okay," he says after a minute. "Okay."

I go into my room and lie on my bed and breathe. I think about the difference between the God I experienced tonight and the God I'd been taught to fear. My mind travels back to the church woman who'd heard the News and said, "God gave you to Craig as his helper. Your duty is to help him through this time." She was right that that is what they taught us at that church: The word the Bible used to name *woman* means *helper.* It was just the religious version of every message I'd ever received from the world—that women are not here to live fully, we are here to help men live fully. Women are supporting actors in the epic stories of men. I think of Liz. *Don't jump through hoops. Walk past the middle men and straight toward the Source.* My eyes fall on the Bible I'd hidden away after the separation—when folks started using it like a cattle prod, to keep me in my place or to push me where they wanted me to be. I walk over and open it and look for the passage, right there in the beginning, where God made man and God made woman and woman was called helper. My stomach turns. Could helper really be God's first name for me?

I take my Bible over to my computer and start searching for meanings to the passage, digging to find information about that one original word, translated over and over to me as *helper.* And there on the screen before me, it appears.

The original Hebrew word for *woman,* a word that is used twice to refer to the first woman, three times to refer to strong military forces, and sixteen times to refer to God, is this:

Ezer.

And the tingly, awake feeling I'd had in the breathing class comes back as I read article after article written by other God smugglers—women who'd started printing their own money instead of waiting in line, other women who'd decided to walk around to the back of the ice cream truck. That translation is wrong, they all tell me. It's wrong. I learn this: "The word *Ezer* has two roots: *strong* and *benevolent.* The best translation of *Ezer* is: *Warrior.*"

God created woman as a Warrior.

I think about the tragedies the women in my life have faced. How every time a child gets sick or a man leaves or a parent dies or a community crumbles, the women are the ones who carry on, who do what must be done for their people in the midst of their own pain. While those around them fall away, the women hold the sick and nurse the weak, put food on the table, carry their families' sadness and anger and love and hope. They keep showing up for their lives and their people with the odds stacked against them and the weight of the world on their shoulders. They never stop singing songs of truth, love, and redemption in the face of hopelessness. They are inexhaustible, ferocious, relentless cocreators with God, and they make beautiful worlds out of nothing. Have women been the Warriors all along?

I was disgusted with Craig for being weak, for failing to fulfill the infallible hero role into which the world and I had cast him. But as I look down at my strong, sober body, I think, *What if I have us cast wrong? What if I never needed Craig to be my hero? What if I don't need Craig to be perfectly strong because I am strong? What if I don't need Craig to love me perfectly because I am already loved perfectly? What if I am the Warrior I need? What if I am my own damn hero?*

Growing up is an unbecoming. My healing has been a peeling away of costume after costume until here I am, still and naked and unashamed before God, stripped down to my real identity. I have unbecome. And now I stand: Warrior. Undressed for battle. Strong and benevolent. Both yin and yang. Complete, not in need of completing. Sent to fight for everything worth having: truth, beauty, kindness, shamelessness, love. To march into pain and love with eyes and heart wide open, to stand in the wreckage and believe that my power, my love, my light, are stronger than the darkness. I know my name now. Love Warrior. I came from Love and I am Love and I will return to Love. Love casts out fear. A woman who has recovered her true identity as a Love Warrior is the most powerful force on earth. All the darkness and shame and pain in the world can't defeat her.

As I think these thoughts, I feel my spine straighten. I drop my breath into my belly, and I laugh.

14

The next week, I pack my bags and fly to Michigan for my biggest speaking event yet. This engagement has been planned for months, born out of the popularity of my book. I feel far too unstable to be exposed to a crowd. I might be a Warrior, but I'm a shaky one. I know that there's no room for my representative on that stage. These people invited me because of the vulnerability in my writing, so I need to show the audience my real self. It feels like especially brutal timing for that.

My sister meets me at the gate, takes my bags, and then handles every detail of the trip so I can focus on my presentation. When they announce my name I climb onstage, ignore the crowd, and seek out my sister's eyes. Her gaze is steady and fierce, her head held high. It's okay, she's saying. No matter what happens up there, we're walking out of here together. Before I begin, I take a deep breath and internalize her confidence. I don't care about anything but making my sister proud. I say to God what I always say to God before I speak onstage, *Okay, I showed up, your turn now.*

My talk is about the mental hospital and how I miss it sometimes. I tell the crowd that I landed there partly because of my addiction, and I landed in addiction partly because of my wiring and partly because of the world's wiring. Very young, I looked out at the scary world and decided I was too broken, too different, to risk revealing my true self to it. I felt too weak to survive the pain I knew was the price of love. So I hid.

I explain that addictions are safe little deadly hiding places where sensitive people retreat from love and pain. No one can touch us there, so we feel protected. But since love and pain are the only things that grow us, we start dying as soon as we hide. The cage I built to protect myself from the world's toxins also stole my oxygen. I didn't know I needed to be seen and known like I needed air.

I tell them that the first time I peeked out of my cage was in the mental hospital. Since it was a smaller world with gentler rules, I felt safe being vulnerable. People wore their scars on the outside, so you knew where they stood. There were no representatives there. It was such a relief to stop acting. There were rules about how to listen well and speak kindly. We learned how to dance and paint and write our feelings instead of eat and drink them. We held hands when we were afraid. I cried when I had to leave. I tell them that twenty years later I still feel naked and overly vulnerable in the big world, so I seek out smaller worlds with kinder rules—places like recovery meetings, my blog community, marriage, friendship, faith, art, family—places where it's safe to be fully human and fully known.

I tell them that I'm finally proud of who I am. I understand now that I'm not a mess but a deeply feeling person in a messy world. I explain that now, when someone asks me why I cry so often, I say, "For the same reason I laugh so often—because I'm paying attention." I tell them that we can choose to be perfect and admired or to be real and loved. We must decide. If we choose to be perfect and admired, we must send our representatives out to live our lives. If we choose to be real and loved, we must send out our true, tender selves. That's the only way, because to be loved we have to be known. If we choose to introduce our true selves to anyone, we will get hurt. But we will be hurt either way. There is pain in hiding and pain outside of hiding. The pain outside is better because nothing hurts as bad as not being known. The irony is that our true selves are tougher than our representatives are. My tender self was never weak at all. She was made to survive the pain of love. My tenderness is my strength. Turns out that I never needed to hide. I was a Warrior all along.

"Thank you for inviting me here," I say. "Thanks for being a safe place to bring my tender, true self."

Then I turn and walk off the stage and out into the brightness of an empty hallway. Somehow, my sister is already there waiting for me. She grabs my shoulders and she says, "You did it. I can't believe you did it. You were so beautiful, so real, so powerful. They're standing up in there. They gave you a standing ovation. You left too fast to see it." She pulls me into her and I start to feel dizzy from adrenaline, relief, and love. I let her hug me and I think, *They gave truth a standing ovation*. "Let's go," she says. "Let's get you something to eat." My sister holds my hands and we walk toward the front doors until we hear a voice behind us.

"Glennon! Glennon! Wait!" We turn around together and see a gray-haired woman hurrying in our direction. When she makes it to us, she says, "Thanks for stopping. I just heard you speak. You were wonderful. I saw in the program that you're from Naples. I used to live there, and I know where you need to go to church. What neighborhood do you live in?" I tell her. Her eyes brighten. "Write this down. It's where you belong. It's just a couple blocks from you, and it's one of those places you spoke about—where it's safe to be fully human."

"Okay! Great! Thank you!" I say. *Hell no,* I think.

I return home the next night and drive slowly through my neighborhood, searching. There, on a corner I've passed a hundred times, stands the church. It's lit up bright against the night sky and I pull over to stare. The white steeple reaches higher than the tallest palm on the grounds. I feel an aching, a yearning to go inside. I see soft yellow light pouring out through a window. I wonder if, on the other side, there's a warm room with flickering candles and Mary waiting for tired night people. I wonder if this is the kind of place I could take off my shoes and feel velvet on the soles of my feet. There are no other cars in the parking lot. I consider that a church without people might be the only safe church for me. But I do not go inside, because I can't risk being sent to the office. Instead I drive home, unpack, snuggle in bed with my computer, and start researching the church's denomination.

I start reading and learn that this was the first church to ordain black and gay ministers. I find a picture of its ministers protesting against mistreatment of immigrants. When I stumble upon picture after picture of these churches flying rainbow flags above their doors, hope stirs inside of me. Judging by the website, this church looks safe, but what I really need to know are the hidden rules. So the following Sunday morning during services, I drive slowly through the church's parking lot, examining the bumper stickers on the cars of the congregation. I find political stickers from both parties. I find environmental stickers and CO-EXIST stickers. I count seven PFLAG stickers. I do not see a single TURN OR BURN sticker, so I decide to give this place a try.

Craig and I go to church together the following Sunday. We're greeted by several snazzy, kind, gray-haired ladies wearing heels, lipstick, and suits. We accept their smiles and church bulletins and head into the sanctuary. Craig motions to a pew in the back and I shake my head and walk straight to the front. Craig follows reluctantly. The organ begins and the first note fills my heart and then the silver-haired choir begins the procession. They are singing an old-fashioned hymn and my heart now feels like a balloon that's floating out of my body. I am trying to regain control because I do not want to be taken for a ride here. *Stay steady,* I tell myself. But then a balding minister rises and starts speaking and he is so gentle and vulnerable that I give up on controlling my heart and just trust it to him for a bit.

This minister declares that he is not here to add barriers between God and people; he's here to remove them. He speaks of the need for a faith that is open and gentle instead of closed and militant. He speaks of his Muslim and atheist and Jewish friends and how each has wisdom he needs. He calls out local and world leaders who spend billions on war and little on peacemaking. He calls out Christians who lobby for tax cuts for the rich and are silent on matters for the poor. He speaks of the candlelight vigil he attended the night before to honor a black teenager who'd just been murdered in a Florida neighborhood while walking his girlfriend home. He calls this death not a misunderstanding, but the direct result of fear mongering and bold-faced racism. He implores his white congregation to consider how it's part of the problem. This sermon is brave. It is relentlessly kind but not at all neutral. I notice that when the minister refers to God, he never uses a pronoun. To him, God is not a man. And when referring to people, he always says "she or he." His language is painstakingly careful. He is speaking a language I recognize as love. Love is careful and love is humble. This man is careful and humble, and he is using his voice to lift to the surface those who've been forgotten. He is using his freedom to go back and fight for those not yet free. The last are first, even in the words he chooses. I do not see any pictures of Mary, but I sense through this minister's language that the divine feminine is present and safe here.

After the service, Craig and I walk out of the sanctuary and a woman approaches us with a sincere and curious smile. As I say hello my eyes fall on the comma-shaped, rainbow-colored pin on her lapel. She notices me noticing it, and as her hand rises to touch the pin she says, "The comma is because God is still speaking. And the rainbow is for the gays, of course."

"Ah," I say, "yes. Of course. Well, I'm here because a lady in Traverse City chased me down and promised that this was the place for a girl like me."

I describe the woman and this rainbow lady says, "That's Kathy! She was a minister here. Amazing, brilliant, strong woman. She was a Catholic nun and then became an Episcopal priest. She marched with Martin Luther King, Jr., you know. Well, welcome. I'm Charnley. Lovely to meet a girl like you." Charnley turns, points to the minister, and says, "That guy is my husband."

I smile. I like that instead of introducing herself as the minister's wife, she calls him her husband. On the way out, Craig looks at me and says, "We are totally coming back here. Don't you think? This place feels right."

"Yes," I say. "Maybe so."

We return the next week and at the end of the service Rev. Ron and another leader, Rev. Bev, announce that they've just hired a third minister named Dawson—a man who preaches like fire and who happens to be gay. This gray-haired congregation has voted him in. They have voted not to tolerate him, not to change him, but to ask him to lead them. As Bev smiles after her announcement and the congregation cheers, I stop holding my breath. I decide to take a risk on this family. Not because I won't get hurt, but because they are the right people to get hurt by. I trust the rules here. After Rev. Dawson is inducted as our minister, I join the congregation officially.

I am still afraid to trust my children to this institution, so I request a meeting with the children's minister, Nancy. She sits with me in her office as I share my fears about what my kids might learn and then have to unlearn about God. I tell her that we need a church that will help us practice loving ourselves without shame, loving others without agenda, and loving God without fear. A church that will give my children and me room to breathe and grow, and will never silence our dissent, doubt, or questions. Nancy listens without judgment. She opens her whole heart and mind to me. When I am done, she says, "Would you help me teach our children? Will you help me teach them the kind of love you just explained to me?" I am shocked, so I just stare at her for a long minute, contemplating her invitation. Finally I say, "Yes. Yes, I will." And that's how I become a minister of the Gospel of love.

Every week, I sit with the children of our congregation and I tell them about the God of the bathroom floor. I tell them that Jesus' way is love and that there are plenty of folks screaming his name who aren't following the way, and that there are plenty of people who've never uttered Jesus' name who are following the way of love beautifully. I teach them that faith is not a club to belong to, but a current to surrender to. I teach them that they'll know they're in the current when they are becoming kinder and gentler and more open and grateful and when they feel constantly carried toward people they fear so they can fall in love and stop being afraid. I teach them that the two most repeated phrases in the Bible are "Do Not Be Afraid" and "Remember." Our human family is dismembered because we have been taught to fear each other. To have peace, we must allow love to bring us back to each other. To Re-member. I promise them that we are just scattered pieces of the same puzzle, so when we hurt each other, we hurt ourselves. I explain that my idea of heaven is the completion of the scattered puzzle—but I ask them not to wait for some otherworldly reunion. I ask them to bring heaven to earth here and now—to invite the Kingdom of God today—by treating every last one of God's people like kin. I tell each of them, *Be brave because you are a child of God. Be kind because everyone else is, too. We belong to each other.*

I teach them that they are loved by God—wildly, fiercely, gently, completely, without reservation. I promise that there is nothing inside of them that they need to be ashamed of. I become a megaphone for the still, small voice that was drowned out so early for me—the voice that says to each of us, *You! You are my beloved! I made you and everything you have ever been or are or will become is already approved. Nothing you can ever do will make me love you more, and nothing you can ever do will make me love you less. That is finished. So stop hiding, stop waiting, and come now! Just get up and dance with me!* Every time I look into a ten-year-old's eyes and promise her that she is good and loved so she never needs to go underneath to breathe, I know I am also speaking to my ten-year-old self. *Don't hide. You are safe here. You belong, precious one, after all. Do not be afraid. Remember.*

Months pass. The kids are in school and suddenly it's fall again, a year since I got the News. I can feel the current softening me and trying to lead me toward Craig. I'm resisting that current hard. I'm afraid to surrender to it. One day, I go to see Ann and I say, "So, I've been thinking. It turns out I'm not Gandhi. Not Elsa either. I'm not a helper and I'm not a canary. I'm actually a Warrior."

She smiles and raises her eyebrows into a question.

I explain: "I've started to think of myself as a triangle—body, mind, spirit." Ann nods, indicating for me to go on. "I'm a trinity, right? So I'm looking at this triangle the other day and thinking of the scriptures about loving God with all our strength, soul, and mind. I feel like I know how to love with my mind and soul. I love with my mind when I write, read, and think. That's my intellectual life. I love with my soul when I pray, meditate, care for others. That's my spiritual life. I've created those lives. They're forged on my terms, not terms that have been given to me by anyone else. But I've been issued this body along with my mind and soul. It makes sense that I should be living and loving with it, too. The problem is that 'loving with my body' makes me think of sex. I'm paralyzed by that thought. I can't imagine ever trusting Craig enough to have sex with him again. Sex has done nothing but hurt me. Why would I go there again? It makes no sense."

Ann thinks about this. "Trust takes time," she replies. "Intimacy between two people is a mountain. Sex is the top and you and Craig are at the base. You can't start by leaping to the top, you two have already tried that once. You missed the climb, and the climb is when you bond. You've got to climb together. One step at a time. First things first. Let's talk about hugging and kissing."

"Okay. Well, I don't like hugging and kissing. Craig's hugs feel stifling to me. I'll be busy doing something and he'll stop me in the middle of the kitchen, grab me, and hold on too tight and too long. His hugs feel more like control or fear to me than love. His hugs feel so needy."

"All right. What about kissing? In the past, what have you been thinking when you and Craig are kissing?"

"What have I been thinking? I've been thinking, Who decided this was a thing? Who was the first person to say 'Oh! I have an idea! Let's put our tongues inside each other's mouths now!' Probably some guy who wanted a woman to stop talking so he could have sex with her. That's what kissing feels like to me: silencing and suspicious. Sex is the end and kissing is the means. Kissing is just a stepping-stone to the next thing a guy wants. I resent it." Ann looks at me, her eyebrows raised again. I add, "I know. I'm a hopeless romantic."

"So while all of this is going on inside of you," Ann says, "what are you communicating? Do you tell Craig how you're feeling, what you're thinking?"

"Of course not. I just wait it out."

"Right. Your feelings and thoughts are valid, Glennon. You're allowed to have them. They make sense and you shouldn't be ashamed of them. But you need to share them with Craig or whomever you're being intimate with. Right then. In the moment. You have to trust your feelings and speak them. When your mind says one thing but your body says another—that's miscommunication, dismemberment. This is about reunion, Glennon. This is where we get your thoughts and actions—your mind and body—to work together. When you feel angry, used, afraid, don't pretend to be otherwise. Tell the truth with all parts of you. There's nothing wrong with how you feel, but there is something wrong with pretending otherwise. Marriage should be a lifetime of learning about each other and developing intimacy minute by minute, not becoming more cut off and alone with each passing day.

"Craig's working hard on this, too. He's practicing using words to speak his needs and feelings instead of just his body. The way you learned sex—dark, shameful, impersonal—that's how Craig learned it, too. You both learned it as a way to use people to get your needs met instead of as a way to give and receive love. You both learned it in dark basements with too much alcohol and shame. That's why there's so much shame involved now. That's why it all feels so wrong to you. There is so much for you two to unlearn. You have had plenty of sex, but neither of you has ever had intimacy with each other—nor have you been intimate with anyone else, for that matter. You are both at the very, very beginning. At the base of the mountain.

"You've told Craig it's all right for him to hug you again. Let's stay at that spot on the mountain for as long as it takes. We'll go slow, so you feel safe. This week I want you to work on hugging. When Craig hugs you, I want you to trust yourself enough to check in with your feelings and thoughts and then share them honestly with Craig."

~

The next afternoon I'm standing on the sidewalk in front of my house, holding my dog's leash. A garbage truck stops across the street and a man hops off the back of the truck, walks over to my neighbor's trash can, and then stops to look at me. The aggressiveness of his eye contact feels both intimate and threatening. I hold my breath. I tell myself to stop being ridiculous, I'm safe. Of course I'm safe. We are twelve feet apart and we are looking right at each other, so I nod to acknowledge him. He looks away from me and back into the cab of the truck. He makes eye contact with the driver, and they smirk at each other. My body stiffens. The man's eyes glisten and he brings his thumb and index finger to his mouth, preparing to wolf whistle at me. He is looking right at me again, but what he's about to do has nothing to do with me. It's not personal. I am just an inside joke between him and the driver. My insides catch fire. I am furious. I'm on my own quiet street, early in the morning, and this man is about to pierce the air at me. I brace myself for the shrill noise about to come, but then I say to myself: *Tell the story of your insides with your voice.* I remember that what I think I should or should not feel doesn't matter. What matters is how I actually feel and that I don't pretend otherwise. How I feel is afraid and angry. How I feel is that this is utter horseshit; a woman should be able to walk her damn dog without being harassed by a stranger. How I feel is tired of being afraid of men. So right there on the sidewalk in front of my home, I host a reunion. Instead of turning away, I look as intently as I can into the man's eyes and I point at him with my free hand and I say loudly, "No. Don't. Don't do that. Don't do that to me."

I am stunned by the ferocity and steadiness of my own voice. I am the one who has pierced the air and now he is the one who is frozen. He drops his fingers. We look at each other for a moment and play a game of chicken. I do not look away. He does. Then he says, "I'm sorry, ma'am." I breathe and nod again. He turns away from me, dumps my neighbor's can into his truck, climbs onto the back, and hits the truck's metal side with his fist. This is the driver's signal to drive away. I watch them go. The air is quiet again.

I look around and I am still on my own street in front of my own house walking my own dog. I did not abandon myself. Instead, I announced and honored myself. In honoring myself, I also honored the man and the space between us. I reminded him that we were both human. I looked into his eyes and said, *Here I am. I am in here. I am more than you can see. I am a soul and a mind, as well as a body—and all of me is saying no. Don't do that to me.* I looked into a man's eyes and introduced myself. And in that introduction, he remembered, too. He saw himself in me, and that is why he dropped his fingers. His eyes said, *Pardon me. I did not realize you were in there.* I stood on the street in the quiet and I wondered, *If I can do this with a stranger, can I also do this with my husband?*

~

Later that evening, while I am doing the dishes, Craig comes up behind me, puts his arms around me, and holds me still. I feel hope and fear in his arms. I wait it out for a few moments but he doesn't let go and I don't like it. It's too much, too fast. I didn't ask for this hug. My insides are speaking to me, so I speak them to Craig. While his arms are wrapped around me I say into the sink, "I know you are trying to be loving, but this doesn't feel like love to me. I want to be invited to affection, not ambushed by it. When you grab me I feel resentful and annoyed and then I feel like a bitch for feeling that way. This cycle isn't good for either of us. I need you to understand and respect the way I'm wired. You can't just pounce on me. Also, I need you to stop holding me so tight. I feel like you're trapping me so I can't decide to end this. I feel like you are taking my power. I'm smaller than you and I don't want to think about that every time we hug."

I stand and stare out the window and wait for the world to crumble because I've just admitted out loud that I have ice running through my veins. I've just disturbed all the unspoken rules of the universe about how peace depends upon a woman's agreement to suffer small and large indignities with a smile. I have broken the code that insists I just be grateful for whatever I get and pretend to need love more than I need freedom. But as I stand there, I feel a thrill mixed with my fear. I've wanted to say these words since I was fifteen years old. And there I am. I've just introduced myself. I might be a bitch, but I'm free. I've gotten my insides out and I allow myself to consider that maybe my inside feelings are valid, simply because they are mine.

I wonder if there's nothing horribly wrong with me after all. Maybe I'm just a woman who, because of her wiring, likes to be hugged a certain way. Maybe it makes sense for her husband to know that about her. Maybe he'd *want* to know because he'd want her to feel safe and loved and happy. Or maybe not. Maybe he already knows and has decided that his needs are more important.

He could resent me for everything I've just said. But as Craig removes his arms from my waist I think, *I'd rather lose him forever than lose myself ever again. I will never abandon myself again. That is all I know.* This thought surprises and scares and comforts me. *Here I am, Craig. This is the real me. The real me doesn't like the way you've been hugging me. I'd rather you resent me for who I really am than love me for who I'm not.*

I'm still facing the sink when Craig says, "It makes sense that you feel all that. Right before I hugged you I saw you there and felt scared. I'm so afraid of losing you. Every day, I'm afraid you're going to leave. I just want to hold on to you. I should have told you how I was feeling instead of grabbing you."

~

The next morning, Craig slips a note onto my desk that says: "Hi! Meet me in the kitchen at 1:00 for a lunch hug?" At first I feel humiliated that our relationship has come to this. *Index-card hug invitations?* But then I feel relief that our relationship has come to this. I feel safe. I feel like what I want and need matters. At 1:00 I go to the kitchen and Craig looks at me and says, "Thanks. I won't ask anything else from you. Just be here with me for a minute." He opens his arms and I snuggle into him. He holds me loosely, so I have plenty of room to breathe. After a moment he lets go completely so that I can decide when the hug will end. I let go, too. The whole process is awkward, but safe. We are being careful with each other.

A few days later, I find another note on my desk. It's written on the kids' construction paper and it's decorated with Tish's stickers. It's an invitation from Craig to a real date. The invite indicates that a babysitter has been arranged and a reservation has been made, but both can be canceled if I'm not ready. Craig has drawn three boxes and asked me to check one. My choices are yes, no, or maybe. I check yes and leave the invitation on Craig's desk.

As soon as we sit down to dinner on date night, I can tell that Craig has been learning how to ask better questions. First, he asks me how a specific work relationship is going, and then he asks about an old friend going through chemo. When I answer, he's listening carefully—like he understands that I'm giving him a gift he should handle with care. We are sitting across from each other at the table and we are both present in the space between us. It feels new. Even so, we're both relieved to get back home, because the couch is the best part of any date. We let the babysitter go, change into our pajamas, and turn on the TV. I lie next to Craig and he turns his head to look at me. We are close to each other and he is looking right into my eyes and my insides start squirming. Steady eye contact has always felt nosy and controlling to me, like someone is looking a little too hard for my real self whether or not I'm ready to present her. This eye contact with Craig makes me lose my boundaries, it makes me feel woozy and out of control, so I prepare to break it. I decide to pat Craig on the shoulder and look away, back at the television where it's safer. Then I remember the Journey of the Warrior. *Be Still. Don't jump off your mat. Don't run out of here. If you can sit with the hot loneliness for 1.6 seconds . . .* I keep looking into Craig's brown eyes and I feel fluttery and light-headed. It's like quiet and music used to be, almost unbearable. Until something inside of me shifts.

All of a sudden I feel the desire to kiss Craig. I can't believe that this is true, but I check in with my body and find that indeed, it is. My mind starts to panic. I can most certainly *not* kiss Craig because a kiss is an open door to more. A kiss would be removing all the steel bars that I've forged to keep me safe. I feel myself dismembering. I am no longer in my eyes, in Craig's eyes, nor am I in the space between us. I am back in my own head. But instead of staying lost in there alone, I invite Craig in. I tell the story of my insides with my voice. I say, "I feel like kissing you right now, but I'm afraid to because I don't want things to go any further. I need to be the one to initiate every new step."

"Okay," he says. "I understand what you're saying. I won't try anything new. Never again, unless you tell me different. I want you to feel safe." And so I kiss Craig. And there on that couch in our pajamas, just for a few moments, we fall into love.

15

THE SUN SHINES WARM and the wind blows cold on the first day of spring—my thirty-eighth birthday. It's been eighteen months since Craig delivered the News, twelve since he moved back home. I squint into the bright morning and try to find Amma's soccer jersey on the field. There she is, number ten, trying hard to appear involved while skillfully avoiding any actual involvement with the game. Her eyes track the ball and every few moments she yells, "Get it!" But the permanent twenty-foot span between her and the ball makes it clear to her teammates that she will not be the one getting it. During breakfast that morning, Amma admitted what we already knew: She doesn't like soccer after all. She explained that there was just too much kicking. I asked Amma if she'd like to stop playing and she said no, she would continue on valiantly because of the snacks. I thought this made for a pretty decent philosophy. Life: lots of scary kicking made bearable by snacks. Perhaps Craig is right, valuable life lessons can be learned from sports.

Coach Craig paces the sideline while studying his elf-size players. He stands taller and more confidently on the soccer field than he does anywhere else. He laughs and offers a thumbs-up to one of his players who just scored a goal for the other team. He runs onto the field to retie three sets of muddy shoelaces. He calls out, "Drew! The game is happening! No climbing the goal now!" And, "Play now, Sophia! Hug later!" I watch the faces of the clapping parents and note that they seem relaxed and entertained. The kids on the field are ecstatic, proud—not a sign of stress on any of their faces. I turn back toward Craig and see his tan arms crossed over his chest and his whistle swinging easily around his neck. I think, *He's like a conductor. All of this running, kicking, shouting, and interrupting should feel like chaos, but under Craig's kind, skillful leadership it all seems to work together, like a symphony. And for the love of God, Coach Craig is gorgeous over there.*

Earlier in the season, the mother of one of Amma's teammates nudged me and said, "This is my friend, Joanne. She doesn't have kids on this team, she just comes to watch Coach Craig. Aren't we the luckiest soccer moms ever?" Then she winked at me. Since then, I've avoided Craig after games so this poor woman doesn't die of embarrassment when she learns that Coach Craig is my husband. But now I notice that this isn't a fluke; all the moms are beaming at Craig. Of course they are. He's handsome and gentle and he adores their kids. What's not to beam about?

Amma's team loses the game by seven goals, but Craig doesn't seem to mind as his players huddle around him for their postgame pep talk. He crouches down while they maneuver as close to him as possible. A little girl with shiny black curls snuggles onto his left knee and I watch Amma flop with a flourish onto his right. She wraps her arms around Craig's neck like a jealous monkey, claiming him. Craig kisses her forehead and then reaches around her to high-five the rest of the team. I draw a bit closer along with the other moms. One of them catches my eye and winks at me. I decide that is really quite enough with the winking. I concentrate on resisting the urge to muscle my way into the huddle to claim my own section of Craig's lap. Suddenly, I imagine pulling Craig toward me and kissing him tenderly. I feel a warmth, a stirring. The feelings travel down through my body. Then the vision and feeling evaporate and I stand there stunned and disoriented.

After a loud "Go team!" Amma and her teammates run off with their orange slices while Craig prepares to coach Chase's team. From a distance, I watch Craig peel off his first coaching jersey to replace it with another. I feel shocked to suddenly see—right there in the light of day—Craig's stomach and chest. They are smooth and toned and completely exposed. A teeny electrical current runs through my body. I feel like running across the field to him, placing my hands on his chest, and yelling to all the beaming mamas, *That's my man!* Wait, what? MY MAN? Who AM I? A jealous teenager at the food court? I feel baffled at myself. Within the span of an hour I've experienced pangs of jealousy, teeny electrical currents, and sudden kissing visions. And now I feel this . . .

powerful stirring. This being moved, awakened, which feels like a low tingling. It feels like my body is tugging at me, the same way my kids do when they need something from me. My body is saying to me, *I want something.* I've practiced enough to know how to listen. But what does my body want? Craig?

Months ago, when Ann asked me, "What is attractive to you about Craig?" I'd stared at her blankly. She changed her wording. "Okay, what do you *respect* about Craig?" I'd been unable to answer either question. I'd lost respect for Craig, so I'd lost attraction. I wonder now if this low tingling is a signal that I've recovered some of both. I look over at him and wonder, *What do I respect about him right now?* Maybe I respect his coaching? He's confident here. A leader. Could be that. Maybe it's his kindness to the kids and parents? His patience and easy laugh? Then I look at him and think, *Wait, is it the coaching and kindness, or is it just the abs? Can a woman respect abs?*

I watch him in the circle with Chase and the boys and I think, *I know what I respect:* Look at him. There he is. He didn't jump off his mat and run out of here. He messed everything up and then he stayed and fought through his pain and my pain and the kids' pain and he let none of it scare him away. He chose the Journey of the Warrior, too—and so there he is, still in the middle of his life. He became his own hero. He was his hero and I was mine and now here we are, together. Two heroes. Not two halves that make one whole, but two wholes that make a partnership. *That's attractive.*

My mind travels back to my wedding day. I see myself walking down the aisle toward Craig. There he is, standing with the minister. He's smiling, but he is so clearly afraid. He is not ready. Are we ever ready for the terrifying gifts life offers us? I can see now that he is, as he stands there in his tuxedo costume, everything I hate: uncertain, weak, dishonest, unhealthy. But he is also everything that I love. He is hopeful. He is brave. He is afraid, but he has shown up anyway. He is human. I didn't want him to be human. I wanted him to be perfect and golden, steady and solid, simple and strong so that I could be messy, complicated, and weak. But we are each all of those things. "I just need to know if you can really know me and still love me," he had said to me in his therapist's office. I think about my parents sitting on the couch, betrayed, terrified, exhausted, saying to me, "Do you even love us, Glennon?" *Yes. Yes I did.* I, of all people, understand that you can love someone so much it aches and still hurt them, again and again. I know that you can love and betray the very same person. Is it possible that I walked down the aisle toward exactly the right person? Toward my healing partner? Toward myself?

When I got to the end of that aisle, Craig took my hand. He knew my mess and he married me. I thought he was perfect and I married him. Who was braver? In my mind's eye I watch us take each other's hands. I feel so tender. This is the first tenderness I've felt in so long. Tenderness and respect mixed together feel a lot like love.

I'd been angry and ashamed because my marriage was so far from perfect. But perfect just means: *works exactly the way it is designed to work.* If marriage is an institution designed to nurture the growth of two people—then, in our own broken way, our marriage is perfect.

~

This thought enters my mind: *I am going to have sex with Craig today.* It is going to be my idea. This is a decision delivered from my body to my mind and soul. My body has joined us as a decision maker. I feel a wave of terror. What if my body is trying to betray me again? Can I trust my body? What if it tells me to give myself up and he throws it all away again? Then this answer from my mind: *What he does with my love is neither my problem nor my concern.* My body wants to offer and receive love and I am going to listen. This is not just about trusting Craig, this is about trusting myself.

Later that afternoon, Craig drops the kids off to play at a neighbor's house and then he comes back home to take a shower. While he showers, I sneak into the bedroom, peel off my clothes, and jump into bed. I hide all the way under the covers so Craig won't know I'm there. I feel ridiculous and reckless under there. When I hear him come out of the bathroom and start making his way across the room, I peek out from under the covers and make a high-pitched noise, like a mouse. *Good God, I am five years old.* Craig looks over at me, sees me under the covers, and raises his eyebrows. He says, "Hey. What's going on?"

"I don't know," I reply. "I'm in here. I'm under the covers." This is not sexy, I think. This is definitely not sexy.

But what the hell does *sexy* even mean? I wonder if the word sexy is everything that made sex a lie to me. Sexy meant grown women acting like lingerie is just what we want for Valentine's Day even though it's obviously wrapping paper for a gift our husbands want returned to them later. Sexy was pretending not to be hungry. Sexy was bleach and heels and bending over pool tables and other uncomfortable things. Sexy was one type of body and one color of hair and spending an entire life looking into a mirror instead of out at the world. Sexy was what marketers told me was sexy so I'd buy whatever they were selling. I'd been trying to be that kind of sexy for twenty years, and lying there in bed, I realize that's going to have to change. That definition of sexy is what poisoned my husband and me and it's never going to work for us again. I am going to have to try to have sex without any fake, commercial sexiness involved. Maybe it's possible that I don't have to hate sex just because I hate the world's definition of sexy. Maybe I can find my own sexy.

Craig keeps standing there, waiting for me to speak. It's been a year and a half since we've really touched each other, and we've never touched each other as the new people we are now. I see the fear on his face and feel my own fear. I remind myself that scared and sacred are sisters. "It's okay, I'm scared, too. Come here," I squeak.

"I can't come there," Craig says as he points to his towel. "I'm naked under here."

"I know," I say. "It's okay." He walks over slowly, drops his towel on the floor, and scrambles into bed with me. Side by side, we hug. It's a gentle, loose hug—like we've practiced. I notice that we're both shaking. That feels honest. I wonder if shaking is my kind of sexy. I look over Craig's shoulder and out the open window. Birds are chirping. It's sunny and bright. Nothing feels dark, scary, sinister, or dirty. We are out in the open, in the light. I silently beg God to show up. *Please, God, make it different this time. Help. If it's not different I'm afraid it will all be over. Not just for us, but for me. Please come in and help us with this.* I take a few deep breaths. I am here. I am in my body. I've remembered.

Then we kiss. And the miracle that happens is this: I stop wondering things. My brain changes modes. I do not hover. I am not God. I am just human, so I can let go and be present and surrender to this, whatever it is. I show up. Mind, body, spirit—all of me, at once.

I hear myself say things. Not stupid fake things like I'd learned from movies, like: "Oh my God" and "Yeah, baby," but real things—things I'd learned to say from all the hugging practice. I speak my insides. I say, "Slow down. Stay there." There is one horrifying moment in which Craig pulls away from me and closes his eyes and I can feel him dismembering. As soon as he disappears, I do, too. I think, *If you leave right now, if you close your eyes and pull away and it becomes clear that your mind is with the stilettoed ladies and not with me, I swear this will never happen again. I swear to God if I feel you leave this place I will. . . .* Suddenly, I am alone again. I am alone with my fear in my mind. I am two people: me on the outside having sex, and me on the inside all alone. I know I have to tell the story of my insides with my voice if I want to stay whole. No abandoning myself. So I say, "No, don't. Come back.

You're scaring me. Stay here. All of you. Stay here." I pull Craig back toward me and he holds me lightly but closely and he is suddenly back. I can tell. We are both back from the alone and we are together. He is not with the stilettoed ladies and their version of sexy. He is here, with me and my version of sexy, which is: *After all of this, I am trying again. I am trying. I am still here. All of me.*

And for a few moments there is a meeting of two bodies. And for a few moments there is a meeting of two minds. And for a few moments there is a meeting of two souls, with no lies between them.

Here I am. Here you are. All of me. All of you. Here. In love.

Afterward, we lie in bed and breathe together for a bit. And I look over at Craig and see tears running down his face. There he is. All of him, right at the surface so I can see him.

"That felt different," Craig says.

"Yeah," I say. "That felt like love."

Amma shimmies around the kitchen with one hand on her hip and the other on the back of her head. She strikes several suggestive poses while shouting, "I'm sexy and I know it. Oh yeah, oh yeah!" I recognize this as the chorus to a recent pop song. I stare at Amma and wonder, *Where exactly does a kindergartner learn to arrange her hands and shake her hips like that?* An observer would be forgiven for thinking we spend family night at the local strip club. Amma stops dancing long enough to study the question on my face. She says proudly, "Beyoncé, Mama. I learned this dance from Beyoncé." I hear Craig laugh in the other room. We are all suckers for Beyoncé.

Tish, the morality cop of the family, bounds into the room, and like a referee throwing a flag onto the football field, she yells, "Inappropriate, Amma! Sexy is inappropriate!"

Amma yells back, "No, it's not!"

Tish says, "Yes it is! Sexy IS inappropriate, right, Mom?"

I freeze. This argument sounds very much like the civil war that has raged in my mind for the last two decades. Is sexy inappropriate? Is sexy wrong? Is sex wrong? It can't *be* wrong, but how can something that has forever been twisted to subjugate women not *feel* wrong? My girls stare at me, waiting for the verdict. Delivering it feels above my pay grade. This moment feels heavy with meaning—as if my response might determine the kind of women these girls become. *How can a woman who's been so confused about her body and sex for so long lead her girls toward healthy relationships with sex? How can I possibly be the right person for moments like these? What is the right answer here?*

I look down at my girls' expectant faces and I remember that there is no right answer. There are only stories to tell. Every day the world will tell my girls its story about sexiness and what it means to be a woman. My girls need to hear my story. Not so my story will become theirs, but so they'll understand that they are free to write their own stories. They need to know that much of what the world presents to them is not truth, it's poison. And my girls will only be able to detect lies if they know what truth sounds like. I take a deep breath and tell myself to relax. This is just the beginning of a lifelong conversation the three of us will have about womanhood.

I say, "You know, I think sexy is good. It's just that most people are confused about what it means. Want to know what sexy really means?"

Yes, they nod. Their wide eyes say, *I can't believe Mom keeps saying sexy.*

"I think sexy is a grown-up word to describe a person who's confident that she is already exactly who she was made to be. A sexy woman knows herself and she likes the way she looks, thinks, and feels. She doesn't try to change to match anybody else. She's a good friend to herself—kind and patient. And she knows how to use her words to tell people she trusts about what's going on inside of her—her fears and anger, love, dreams, mistakes, and needs. When she's angry, she expresses her anger in healthy ways. When she's joyful, she does the same thing. She doesn't hide her true self because she's not ashamed. She knows she's just human—exactly how God made her and that's good enough. She's brave enough to be honest and kind enough to accept others when they're honest. When two people are sexy enough to be brave and kind with each other, that's love. Sexy is more about how you feel than how you look. Real sexy is letting your true self come out of hiding and find love in safe places. That kind of sexy is good, really good, because we all want and need love more than anything else.

"Fake sexy is different. It's just more hiding. Real sexy is taking off all your costumes and being yourself. Fake sexy is just wearing another costume. Lots of people are selling fake sexy costumes. Companies know that people want to be sexy so badly because people want love. They know that love can't be sold, so they have big meetings in boardrooms and they say, 'How can we convince people to buy our stuff? I know! We'll promise them that this stuff will make them sexy!' Then they make up what sexy means so they can sell it. Those commercials you see are stories they've written to convince us that sexy is the car or mascara or hair spray or diet they're selling. We feel bad, because we don't have what they have or look how they look. That's what they want. They want us to feel bad, so we'll buy more. It almost always works. We buy their stuff and wear it and drive it and shake our hips the way they tell us to—but that doesn't get us love, because none of that is real sexiness. People are even more hidden underneath fake sexiness, and the one thing you can't do if you want to be loved is hide. You can't buy sexy, you have to become sexy through a lifetime of learning to love who God made you to be and learning who God made someone else to be."

My girls are quiet, listening. I study their faces as they study mine. Amma tilts her head and says, "Oh. I thought sexy meant pretty."

"Hmm, nope. Pretty is another thing that can be sold. What and who is pretty is also something those people in boardrooms decide. It's always changing. So if what you want to be is pretty, you'll have to keep changing yourself constantly—and eventually you won't know who you are.

"What I want to be, girls, is beautiful. Beautiful means 'full of beauty.' Beautiful is not about how you look on the outside. Beautiful is about what you're made of. Beautiful people spend time discovering what their idea of beauty on this earth is. They know themselves well enough to know what they love, and they love themselves enough to fill up with a little of their particular kind of beauty each day."

"Like when I dance!" Amma says, spinning and twirling around me.

"Yes. Like when you dance. Many of the things you see me do each day, I do to be beautiful. It's why I take time out to spend with good friends. It's why I read and look at art and always have music I love playing in the house. It's why I light candles in every room. It's why I watch you climb our banyan trees in the front yard. It's why I roll around on the floor with the dogs and why I'm always smelling the top of your heads. It's why I drag you to watch the sunset each week. I'm just filling up with beauty, because I want to be beautiful. You girls are beauty to me, too. When you smile at me, I can feel myself filling."

The girls look at each other, giggle and beam.

"You two will meet plenty of people who are pretty but haven't yet learned how to be beautiful. They will have the right look for the times, but they will not glow. Beautiful women glow. When you are with a beautiful woman you might not notice her hair or skin or body or clothes, because you'll be distracted by the way she makes you feel. She will be so full of beauty that you will feel some of it overflow onto you. You'll feel warm and safe and curious around her. Her eyes will twinkle a little and she'll look at you really closely—because beautiful, wise women know that the quickest way to fill up with beauty is to soak in another human being. Other people are beauty, beauty, beauty. The most beautiful women take their time with other people. They are filling up.

"Women who are concerned with being pretty think about what they look *like*, but women who are concerned with being beautiful think about what they are looking *at*. They are taking it all in. They are taking in the whole beautiful world and making all that beauty theirs to give away to others. Does that make sense?"

Tish says, "I think so. It's like, when you first wake up, Mommy. You look really, really bad. Your hair is messy and your face looks weird. But when you see me, your eyes get twinkly. Is that because you think I'm beauty?"

"Yes, baby. I'm filling up with you. Because I want to be beautiful."

The kids nod and pretend to understand every word I've said. Then Chase calls out for them and Amma pinches Tish and they all run outside. I stand at the counter, listening to the echo of what I've just said to my girls. I consider the possibility that I've been right and wrong my whole life. I was right to want to be beautiful and sexy; I was just wrong to have accepted someone else's idea of what those words mean. It strikes me that I need to throw out the dictionary the world gave me about what it means to be a mother, a wife, a person of faith, an artist, and a woman and write my own. I've finally unlearned enough. I have unbecome, and I am ready to begin again.

I pour myself a cup of tea and stand still in the kitchen. I look down at my hands cupped around my mug and my belly grazing the counter. I say to my body, *I'm sorry. This is me, making amends. I am going to love you now because you are the vessel through which the world delivers beauty and love and wisdom to my soul. My eyes take in the beauty of the Gulf, my lungs take in the freedom of the air, my mouth and stomach accept life from food and drink, my arms gather the love of my children, and my breasts, legs, and hands accept and return the love of my husband. You are the ship that delivers love from the shore of another being to the shore of me. I was an island before. I didn't know how to let myself out or let others in. Thank you. Thank you for accepting all this love and beauty on my soul's behalf. Thank you for being so patient with me.*

Suddenly I find myself wanting more beauty, more love—as if gratitude immediately widened the vessel, creating space for more. I walk out of the kitchen and into my bedroom. I look over at my bed and feel warmth. I ask my body what it needs to feel safe and loved. I think of my senses, and I light some incense. The smell of incense reminds me of holy things, and certainly sex is that. I open the windows so the birds' songs can remind me that what is about to happen was made by God and blessed by God and that any shame added to it is a lie.

Then I walk into the bathroom and wash all the war paint off of my face. I stop to look in the mirror and notice the untouched gray streak running through my short hair. I feel like my gray hair and bare face make me look young. Fresh. Vulnerable and unsure. The woman in the mirror looks unfamiliar, but it's clear that she's not acting. I like her. I step back and look at my body. I look at the stretch marks from carrying my babies and breasts made limp from feeding them. Marks of the Warrior. There's nothing here but what nature insists upon. This is me. Naked, unashamed, stripped down to my barest essentials. Just me. Just me is all I'll ever offer anyone again. Thank God, just me is what Craig needs.

I lie down in bed and invite Craig in. He climbs in next to me, slowly, carefully, reverently. Then we begin the dance of surrender. I let myself respond to Craig's body instinctually—my body and soul and mind moving in synch—like a school of fish that magically turns away and toward the current simultaneously and without caucus. They just know what to do. They have faith. And here I am, present with Craig. Mind, body, soul—showing up. Right here, right at the surface. All of me, in love.

Afterword

CRAIG AND I STAND ON THE BEACH, facing the Gulf of Mexico. The sun is setting and the sky is purple and orange and the water is every shade of blue. I am wearing cutoffs, a tank top, and a ponytail. Craig is in a T-shirt and board shorts. We are both barefoot and the sand is warm on top and cool underneath. We bury our feet deep and we turn toward each other and hold hands. We look into each other's eyes and smile. There is no one else present. No minister, no parents, no children. This is not a show. This is just us. We exchange our new vows.

I say to Craig, "Here I am, Craig."

Craig smiles and says, "Here I am, Glennon."

We kiss—and here we are.

Here we are, and here we vow to be—our true selves right at the surface. Togetherness is what Craig and I have chosen today. Tomorrow, if wisdom leads us in a different direction, we will not be destroyed. We know now that life offers us many paths. Each has its own particular beauty and pain. Each path is love, and at the end of each path is redemption.

I do not know whether we will spend our lives married or loving each other from a distance, but I now know the path of the Love Warrior: I will not betray myself. I will trust the wisdom of the still, small voice. I will not let fear drown her out. I will trust her and I will trust myself.

Love, Pain, Life: I am not afraid. I was born to do this.

Acknowledgments

Craig, for becoming your own hero, so that Here We Are.

Sister Amanda, for coming back for me, for carrying me, following me, leading me, and being my partner since the day you were born.

Amy, for your Warrior heart, for your relentless devotion to the forgotten, for being our third sister.

Mom, for teaching me that love is a relentless showing up for our people. I became like you after all, thank God.

Dad, for teaching me that I have Warrior blood running through my veins. You were right: It's All Okay.

Chase, for bringing me into the world, for being the wisest one I know, for forgiving us, for believing in us still.

Tish, for showing me my own beauty by showing yours, for your elegance and grit and stunning honesty, for your kindness, which is my favorite kind of courage.

Amma, for loving us all so freely and fiercely, for always saying, *I love you, too, Mama,* for the smell of your hair and neck: the most comforting thing I know.

John and Jeffrey, for the true partnership that allows Sister Amy to be true to their callings.

Bobby and Alice, for making us so happy.

Josh, Drew, and Nathan, for encouraging your mama, Amy, to take her part in a world-changing story, for being and believing.

Aunt Peggy, for being our rock and our pilot.

Uncle Keith—now you'll know which page to sign.

Allison, for your sharp mind, for taking a chance, for being our only cool.

Liz B., for your relentless devotion and bottomless heart.

Katherine, Nicol, Meghan, Erin, Natalie, Karen, Tamara, Christine, and Ashley, for the countless hours of love work that have changed the world.

Amy P., for loving through that lens.

Whit, for your tirelessness, brilliance, and devotion, and for believing in me first. For all of those early-morning e-mails: *You're doing it, G! This is it! Keep going!* There is no end to my gratitude. We were meant for each other.

Flatiron—Bob, Liz, Marlena, Molly, Karen, and Emily—for changing publishing with your courage and innovation and dedication. I can't imagine having trusted anyone else with this story.

MARGARET, for taking me on and then taking me everywhere. We have only just begun.

KATHLEEN, for treating our people like family. For becoming family to us.

JENNIFER, for your vision and fire.

JOANNA, for honoring your gift by using it even when no one was watching. For being brave enough to say yes. For being the only artist who could have brought our Love Warrior to life.

~

SARAH, for promising me it was beautiful enough.

SISTER LIZ, for loving and Sistering both of me: Tempest and Honeyhead.

ROB, for the phone call I'll never forget.

BRENÉ AND CHERYL, for bringing the light.

BRIAN AND RACHEL, for keeping the faith and leading with courage and tenderness.

ANN, NIKI, AND PARNASSUS, for holding a cozy corner for me.

NANCY, for a heart so big it became our family's second home.

GOD'S GIRL, for being the world's Love Warrior.

~

MOMASTERY READERS, for doing this brutiful life with me.

TO ALL THE LOVE WARRIORS who have stood with Together Rising: Let's never stop. Let's make Love Win or die trying.